EDWARD SNOWDEN

WHISTLEBLOWER IN EXILE

Enslow Publishing
101 W. 23rd Street
Suite 240
New York, NY 10011
USA

enslow.com

Adam
Furgang

Published in 2019 by Enslow Publishing, LLC.
101 W. 23rd Street, Suite 240, New York, NY 10011

Library of Congress Cataloging-in-Publication Data

Names: Furgang, Adam, author.
Title: Edward Snowden / Adam Furgang.
Description: New York, NY : Enslow Publishing, 2019. | Series: Influential
  lives | Includes bibliographical references and index. | Audience: Grades 7-12.
Identifiers: LCCN 2017016479 | ISBN 9780766092082 (library bound) | ISBN 9781978501720
  (paperback)
Subjects: LCSH: Snowden, Edward J., 1983- —Juvenile literature. | Whistle
  blowing—United States—Juvenile literature. | Leaks (Disclosure of
  information)—United States—Juvenile literature. | Electronic
  surveillance—United States—Juvenile literature.
Classification: LCC JF1525.W45 F87 2018 | DDC 327.12730092 [B] –dc23
LC record available at https://lccn.loc.gov/2017016479

Printed in the United States of America

To Our Readers: We have done our best to make sure all websites in this book were active and appropriate when we went to press. However, the author and the publisher have no control over and assume no liability for the material available on those websites or on any websites they may link to. Any comments or suggestions can be sent by e-mail to customerservice@enslow.com.

Contents

In 2013, Edward Snowden was revealed as the source behind leaks disclosing top-secret mass surveillance programs conducted by the NSA.

Introduction

· · · · · · · · · · · · · · · · · · ·

I magine that you are a professional journalist and that you work for a major news organization. It is your job to research and report about interesting and important stories. You investigate and deliver the truth in the articles you write. Now imagine that a mysterious stranger contacts you via email and tells you that in order to communicate with him further, you will need to encrypt, or secretly code, your email so no one can possibly intercept it and read it. You are not sure what to do so you forget about it for the time being.

Eventually a trusted documentary filmmaker friend of yours asks you to meet her because she has something important to tell you. She requests that you not bring your cell phone. Once you both meet, she quietly explains to you that she has been in contact with someone who is in possession of highly classified files that come from the United States government's most guarded intelligence agency—the National Security Agency (NSA). She then tells you these super secret files reveal that the NSA has been secretly spying on everyone—not just suspected terrorists, but innocent American citizens, too.

Your friend's secret contact then requests that you both to fly to Hong Kong, China, and meet him in a public area of a hotel, in front of a large green plastic alligator. He wants you to be careful and asks you to take precautions. He gives you a secret phrase that you'll exchange when you meet, just so you'll be sure he is whom you've been communicating with all along. Oh, and he also tells you he'll be carrying a toy puzzle—a Rubik's Cube. Once you meet...he'll reveal the rest of the secret NSA files to you.

Your mind is blown. You wonder to yourself if this can possibly be true. Then as you fly to Hong Kong, your friend gives you some of the secret files she received via encrypted emails.[1] The files appear to be genuine, and you realize you are likely sitting atop the biggest scoop of your life.

Does this sound like something from out of a James Bond spy film. Well this is the truth. This is real. And this is exactly what happened to the *Guardian* journalist Glenn Greenwald and documentary filmmaker Laura Poitras. The two eventually met their real-life secret NSA source, Edward Snowden, who gave them, as promised, thousands of top-secret NSA documents. They soon reported on this revelation and blew the lid off the biggest secret mass-surveillance spying program in history.

The *Guardian* first broke the shocking scope of the NSA's surveillance on American citizens in June 2013.

The groundbreaking news was then picked up by media organizations from around the world. Soon afterward, federal prosecutors charged Snowden with theft and espionage, which is spying to obtain military or political secrets.[2] A debate quickly raged through the public and the media. Did Edward Snowden do the right thing by talking to reporters? Is he a hero? Is he a traitor? How did he wind up in Russia? The debates did not just focus on Snowden and end there. The documents Snowden provided to Greenwald and Poitras also directed much scrutiny at the US government itself and the NSA. Reviews on the NSA's surveillance and bulk data collection practices have since taken place, as have some reforms.

Right or wrong, the importance of Edward Snowden cannot be understated. His impact on America's debate over privacy and civil liberties continues to this day.[3] He remains a controversial and important figure, and his story is still ongoing.

CHAPTER ONE

Edward Who?

· ·

You might be familiar with the news reports that someone named Edward Snowden leaked highly classified NSA documents to the media, and in doing so revealed a secret mass-surveillance spying program that shocked every level of our free society. But you are probably wondering: Who exactly is Edward Snowden? Where did he grow up? What was his childhood like? You might imagine that someone who had access to such top-secret sensitive files likely came from a very wealthy and well-connected family, was highly educated with many important degrees, and attended some of the finest schools in the country. The truth about Snowden is remarkable, but likely not in the way that many imagine.

A Young Snowden

Edward Snowden's parents first met when they were teenagers. His father, Lonnie Glenn Snowden Jr., and his mother, Elizabeth Wendy Barrett, married in 1979 when they were both just eighteen years old.[1] Their first child, Jessica, was born a year later. Their second child, Edward Joseph Snowden, was born on June 21, 1983, in Elizabeth City, North Carolina.[2]

Edward Snowden's family has a long history of serving in the government. His father, Lonnie Glenn Snowden Jr., and his grandfather, Lonnie Glenn Snowden Sr., both worked for the United States Coast Guard.[3] Snowden's mother worked in administration and information technology at Baltimore's federal court as the chief deputy clerk. When Edward Snowden was first born, his family lived near the largest Coast Guard air base in the United States.

In 1992, Snowden's father was transferred to a Coast Guard base near Baltimore, and the family moved to Crofton, Maryland, west of Annapolis. Coincidentally, they lived very close to the NSA headquarters at Fort Meade—miles from where Snowden would wind up working years later when he was older. In Crofton, his family lived in a nice house with a two-car garage with a big front lawn

Lonnie Glenn Snowden Jr. defended his son's actions in revealing NSA mass surveillance. He has said that the FBI wanted him to travel to Moscow to convince his son to return to the United States.

in a comfortable middle class suburban neighborhood. Many people who lived there worked for the government. Snowden was nine at the time and his sister was twelve, and they both went to local public schools. Because many people living in Crofton worked for government intelligence, which is the gathering of military or political information, not everyone knew exactly what their parents or their friends' parents did growing up.[4]

Snowden was skinny and shy as a kid, with wispy blonde hair and a happy smile. In a 2013 Fox News interview with Snowden's father, he was described as, "a sensitive, caring young man" who is a "deep thinker" and someone who was "raised to be principled" and "knows the difference between what is just and unjust and right and wrong, and he cares for all people."[5] He also described Snowden as "a principled young man"

The National Security Agency (NSA) headquarters are located in Fort Meade, Maryland. The facility employs as many as 20,000 people. That makes it one of the largest employers in the United States.

who is "very intelligent, very well read." In an article in *Vanity Fair* magazine, his father described him as "a gentle child of exceptional intelligence."[6]

Snowden attended the Anne Arundel County Public School System in Maryland. For a few years, while he attended elementary school and Crofton Middle School, Snowden was in the Boy Scouts. His group, Boy Scout Troop 731, met every week at the Prince of Peace Presbyterian Church.[7] His friends and fellow Boy Scout troop mates recalled Snowden as shy but also happy and friendly.

Brad Gunson grew up near Snowden. He also attended Crofton Middle and Arundel High Schools with Snowden. In a 2013 interview with

> "[Edward] knows the difference between what is just and unjust and right and wrong and he cares for all people."

the *Washington Post,* Gunson recalled Snowden's high voice, feathery blond hair, and obsession with computer video games. "He liked fantasy games, video games," said Gunson.[8]

In high school, Snowden keep mostly to himself but enjoyed computers, tennis, fantasy-based role playing video games, and the popular card game Magic: The Gathering.[9]

To better understand what Edward Snowden was like when he was younger, it can be helpful to consider what it was like for his generation in the years while he was a teenager. Snowden is part of the millennial generation—the generation born between 1980 and 1995. When

Girlfriend Lindsay Mills

When Edward Snowden was about twenty years old, he met Lindsay Mills, who continues to be his longtime companion today. Mills grew up in Laurel, Maryland. According to the *Washington Post,* she attended Laurel High School in Maryland and graduated in 2003. In 2007, she attended the Maryland Institute College of Art. Mills is a performance artist and a dancer who frequently takes photos and posts them online. Mills was depicted in the 2016 Oliver Stone film *Snowden.*

Snowden was growing up as a teen in the 90s, things were very different from the way they are now. Although there were home computers, they were not common then. Cell phones and the internet were also just starting to emerge, but they were not in widespread use by the masses. The original Sony PlayStation video game console was not even released until 1994, when Snowden was eleven.

What was Snowden's favorite music growing up? According to an interview he gave to the British newspaper the *Guardian,* "I've always appreciated electronic music. The melodies I remember with the most fondness are from video games, with a kind of generated 8-bit music."[10]

Snowden also read a lot when he was growing up. He especially enjoyed reading Greek mythology. The ancient myths had a great impact on him, and he relied on their moral messages to help form his own moral conscience. According to *Wired* magazine, Snowden said,

"I remember just going into those books, and I would disappear with them for hours . . . I think that's when I started thinking about how we identify problems, and that the measure of an individual is how they address and confront those problems."[11]

Snowden graduated from junior high school and started his freshman year at Arundel High School in 1997. Then in the fall of his sophomore year (tenth grade) he got sick and came down with mononucleosis. During this illness he was absent for about five months while recovering. At around the same time, his parent's marriage—which was already going through some trouble—began to get worse. A combination of these events may have been contributing factors to him not returning to high school that year.

Edward Snowden grew up in the Anne Arundel County neighborhood of Crofton, Maryland. Snowden attended Arundel High School before dropping out. His home was located at 1419 Knightbridge Turn.

> **"I've always appreciated electronic music. The melodies I remember with the most fondness are from video games, with a kind of generated 8-bit music."**

Snowden was very smart, however, and rather than return and get left back a year, he enrolled in Anne Arundel Community College in 1999. Snowden was just sixteen at the time. While in community college, he took some computer classes and eventually obtained advanced certification as a systems engineer—he would continue on and off with adult education for many years. He also got his GED high school equivalency diploma.

Late Teen Years

The Snowdens went through many changes during Edward's late teens and early adulthood. Elizabeth Snowden filed for divorce from Lonnie Snowden in early 2001. During his parents' bitter break up, Snowden lived with a roommate. His sister, Jessica, went to the University of Maryland and became a lawyer. She is now a researcher for the Federal Judicial Center in Washington, DC. Snowden's father eventually remarried and moved to Pennsylvania. He retired from the Coast Guard in 2009.

In 2002, Snowden's mother bought a condominium in Ellicott City, Maryland, and the two of them lived together there. Snowden spent much of his time there, mostly on the computer, and did not socialize much outside the internet. On the internet, he was much more outgoing. In December 2001, he started chatting online and began posting comments in a technology chat room called Ars Technica. He went by the web username TheTrueHOOHA.[12]

Through the internet, Snowden also became friendly with a group of anime fans. Anime is an extremely popular form of Japanese animation imported into the United States. He would meet up with his anime group of friends near Fort Meade where they would all hang out. According to one of his posts on Ars Technica, he described himself as "without a degree or clearance who lives in Maryland. Read that as 'unemployed.'" He was also interested in Japanese food and dating girls, as well as keeping fit and practicing the martial art Kung-Fu.[15] He also played the Japanese role-playing computer game *Tekken*, and all the while, above all, he continued working and studying the computer. Snowden's aimless years of taking courses, odd jobs, and hanging out would not last forever though.

One of Snowden's friends ran a technology business from a house at Fort Meade, where the NSA is located. Snowden's computer abilities came in handy and he started working for him.

Every American who was old enough to watch the news remembers the 9/11 attacks on the World Trade Center, the Pentagon, and United Airlines Flight 93. The day had a profound impact on the entire United States. Edward Snowden was impacted, too. He was on his way to work at his friend's business when the airplane terrorist attacks on 9/11 occurred.

Lack of Formal Education

Edward Snowden did not graduate from high school or college, but by the time he was twenty-nine years old, he was earning $200,000 a year while working for the NSA-contractor Booz Allen Hamilton.[13] Snowden has since revealed that he regrets dropping out of high school. At sixteen, Snowden took computer courses at Anne Arundel Community College. Over time he enrolled in many courses at various schools, including the University of Maryland's University College and the Computer Career Institute. By 2003, he was also a Microsoft Certified Solutions Expert.[14]

Although staying in school is entirely valuable, there have been many successful people who never finished high school. The billionaire Richard Branson dropped out of school at fifteen, as did David Karp, who started the blogging website Tumblr. Apple Computer founder Steve Jobs, Microsoft's Bill Gates, and Facebook inventor Mark Zuckerberg all dropped out of college and went on to success, fame, and fortune.

And it's not just contemporary successful people leaving school either. Oil tycoon John D. Rockefeller and car manufacturer Henry Ford both left school early and started working age sixteen.

It was at this point that Snowden began to find a direction as he started to consider enlisting in the armed forces. Slowly, he began to steer his life on a course that would lead him to the military, the CIA, and eventually the NSA.

Chapter Two

Military and Intelligence

• • • • • • • • • • • • • • •

Before Edward Snowden contacted journalists Glenn Greenwald and documentary filmmaker Laura Poitras with the intent of leaking NSA documents, he spent a brief period in the military, held several jobs, and traveled to many countries. The path Snowden took and the experiences he had along the way were crucial in his eventual decision to come forward and give up the comfortable life he knew to try to correct what he felt was a moral wrong-doing, unchecked inside the National Security Agency (NSA).

Life in the Military

The idea of a pursuing a career in the government or the military was not an alien concept to Edward Snowden. His father and both his grandfathers had all served in the United States Coast Guard. Snowden's father, Lonnie Glenn Snowden Jr., accomplished the tough task of rising through the ranks of enlisted officers to become a

What Is the NSA?

The National Security Agency is one of the most secretive government agencies in the world. President Harry S. Truman started the NSA on November 4, 1952, realizing that code breaking during World War II helped to win the war. Cracking German and Japanese codes led to many victories against German U-boats, as well as the winning of the Battle of Midway in the Pacific.

The NSA is also a part of the Central Security Service, or CSS. This agency is in charge of collecting and processing intelligence from foreign sources and protects our intelligence from being obtained by foreign sources.

Today, the general public is aware of the NSA and its duties. However, the existence of the NSA was not even known to the public until it was revealed during a Senate investigation in 1975.

warrant officer.[1] He retired in 2009. As well, Snowden's paternal grandfather, Lonnie Glenn Snowden Sr., served in the Coast Guard. Snowden's maternal grandfather, Edward Joseph Barrett, had been a rear admiral and was a flag officer in the United States Coast Guard. He worked as chief of systems for the United States Coast Guard and served until 1999.[2] Barrett then went on to become a senior official with the Federal Bureau of Investigation, or FBI.

The terrorist attacks on September 11, 2001, impacted every American in a very strong way. They

On September 11, 2001, al-Qaeda terrorists hijacked four domestic airplanes, including American Airlines Flight 77, which crashed into the Pentagon, killing 184 people.

· ·

hit particularly close to home for Edward Snowden. His grandfather, Edward Joseph Barrett, was in the Pentagon on September 11, 2001, when a terrorist hijacked airliner crashed directly into the building. Barrett was not injured, but Snowden, who was eighteen at the time, recalled that afternoon to Brian Williams of NBC News in a 2014 interview. "I was on Fort Meade on September 11. I was right outside the NSA . . . So I remember the tension on that day. I remember hearing on the radio the planes hitting, and I remember thinking—my grandfather, who worked for the FBI, was in the Pentagon when the plane hit it. I take the threat of terrorism seriously."[3]

Snowden, like many Americans, felt very patriotic after the terrorist attacks and began to seriously consider a career in the military. In a 2014 interview with *Wired* magazine, Snowden said, "Everybody in my family has worked for the federal government in one way or another. . .I expected to pursue the same path."[4]

After the terrorist attacks of 9/11, the United States became involved in two consecutive wars, both in an effort to fight terrorism. Edward Snowden was keenly aware of the wars and felt the United States was justified in its efforts.

The first war took place in the country of Afghanistan. The United States attack on Afghanistan was called Operation Enduring Freedom, and it began on October 7, 2001. It was fought in an effort to overthrow the Taliban—an extremist quasi-political religious group that had been in power there since the Soviet Union left the country in the mid-1990s. The United States was also in Afghanistan looking for Osama bin Laden, the leader of the terrorist organization al-Qaeda. Bin Laden was the mastermind behind terrorist attacks against the United States, including the ones on September 11, 2001.

> "Everybody in my family has worked for the federal government in one way or another. . .I expected to pursue the same path."

The second war the United States became involved in after 9/11 was in the country of Iraq. The Iraq War was fought in an effort to dismantle Iraq's alleged weapons of mass destruction, as well as its support for terrorist groups such as al-Qaeda. The United States' attack on

Iraq was called Operation Iraqi Freedom, and it began on March 20, 2003.

Eventually, when Snowden was twenty years old, he made the decision to try and join the Special Forces through the 18X program. The 18X program is a US Army Reserve program that began in 2003. The program was created for people who had not completed their education and who had not served in the military to train to become a Special Forces recruits. According to the 18X overview on the goarmy.com website, "Special Forces candidates are given the opportunity to become a member of one of the most highly skilled combat forces in the world. But they must complete and endure the extensive mental/physical training in order to join the Army elite."[5] Snowden hoped that the army's 18X program would give him a path to get recruited eventually by the army's Special Forces if he completed the program. Snowden was also interested in learning foreign languages through the program.[6] The program lasted fourteen weeks and was tough, both physically and mentally. Even after passing the program, selection into the Special Forces was not guaranteed. Snowden joined the army reserves on May 7, 2004, and began his basic training at Fort Benning, Georgia. He found that he was not physically well-suited for the challenges of the program. Things did not go according to plan and he broke both his legs in an accident.[7] Some debate exists regarding whether Snowden did in fact break both his legs.[8] According to a report published by the House Intelligence Committee on September 15, 2016, "He claimed to have left Army basic training because of broken legs when in fact he washed out because of shin splints."[9] On September 28, 2004, Snowden was discharged from the army.

Intelligence

Once Snowden's time in the army was behind him, he spent the next few months without work.[10] In 2005, he began working as a security guard at the University of Maryland's Center for Advanced Study of Language. The top-secret center was affiliated with the NSA and required that Snowden take a polygraph test as well as a background check. Once employed there, Snowden had high-level security clearance. He attended a job fair on intelligence agencies and also did well on aptitude tests, which demonstrated his high level of skills with computers. Snowden's lack of formal education did not stand in his way. He continually demonstrated his advanced skills with computers and this opened doors for him.[11]

In 2006, Snowden was hired by the Central Intelligence Agency and began his career in intelligence. He had top-secret clearance and was sent to Geneva, Switzerland, in 2007 to work undercover as a telecommunications information systems officer. Some of his job duties involved helping to keep the CIA's computer networks secure as well as helping with the security of US diplomats' computers. The job had Snowden living very comfortably. He lived in a big four-bedroom government apartment with a view of the Rhone River and owned a BMW automobile.[12]

It was during this period in Switzerland that Snowden was first exposed to a small slice of how things worked inside the CIA. He did not always like what he was exposed to. Snowden was troubled by one event in which CIA agents attempted to recruit a Swiss banker though nefarious circumstances to gain access to secret banking information. According to Snowden, the banker was given too much to drink and then allowed to drive home. Once he was pulled over for drunk driving, the CIA

1984

George Orwell was an English writer who wrote the dystopian science fiction novel *1984*. The novel was first published in 1949 and depicts a bleak future in the year the novel takes place, 1984. In this fictional future, an authoritarian government controls everything, and every person is constantly monitored and watched electronically. The government in the story is led by an omnipresent leader, Big Brother. The phrase "Big Brother is watching" is a reminder to citizens that they are being watched.

Today, *1984* is recognized as one of the greatest novels of the twentieth century. It can be argued that much of what Orwell predicted in the novel has come true today. We now have computers that have cameras and microphones that can be tapped by outside government security agencies. In 2017, the novel *1984* saw a resurgence in popularity and became a best seller, almost seventy years after it was first published.

stepped in to smooth things over and gain the banker's confidence and eventually his cooperation. According to a quote from Snowden in the book *The Snowden Files: Inside the Story of the Worlds' Most Wanted Man*, "Much of what I saw in Geneva really disillusioned me about how my government functions and what its impact is in the world. I realized that I was part of something that was doing more harm than good."[13]

> "I realized that I was part of something that was doing more harm than good."

Snowden moved to the global communications division at the CIA headquarters in Langley, Virginia, where he became increasingly unhappy working for the CIA. In one incident, Snowden added some computer code into an application, which ended up having flaws and susceptibility to hacking. Despite getting clearance, he was still reprimanded by a superior for the incident. According to a 2013 article in the *New York Times*, "his supervisor wrote a derogatory report in his personnel file, noting a distinct change in the young man's behavior and work habits, as well as a troubling suspicion." Snowden left the CIA in February 2009.[14]

Any suspicions the CIA had about Snowden did not follow him to his next job. He went on to work as a private contractor for the computer company Dell. It assigned him to a military base in Japan that was being used as a NSA facility. Because Snowden already had a fondness for anime and other Japanese culture, working in Japan was a dream come true for him. He was stationed near Tokyo

The lobby of CIA headquarters in Langley, Virginia, displays a large granite seal on the floor. The large sixteen-foot-diameter emblem has been the symbol of the CIA since 1950. Edward Snowden worked for the CIA from 2006 to 2009.

at the Yokota Air Base. His job there was to help keep officials' computer networks safe from Chinese hacking.[15] Snowden's in-demand computer skills allowed him to receive attractive job offers all over the world. He eventually left Japan in 2012 for another attractive position in Hawaii, where he worked as a system administrator for the NSA.[16] In Hawaii, Snowden was exposed to top-secret files, information, and evidence of mass surveillance that disturbed him greatly. It was during this period that Snowden began to conceive his plan to become a whistleblower and release secret files to journalists. In March 2013, Snowden began working for another NSA contractor, Booz Allen Hamilton. Snowden's next decisions—stemming from a crisis of conscience—would be ones that would irrevocably change his life. He would leave his girlfriend, family, friends, and even his country. He would also leave his job and would give up his big salary. His next stop was a hotel room in Hong Kong.

CHAPTER THREE

Hong Kong

• • • • • • • • • • • • • •

In March 2013, the director of national intelligence, James Clapper, appeared before Congress in a public hearing. Senator Ron Wyden of Oregon asked Clapper a direct question about mass surveillance. He asked, "Does the NSA collect any type of data at all on millions, or hundreds of millions, of Americans?" Clapper responded, "No, sir . . . Not wittingly. There are cases where they could inadvertently, perhaps, collect. But not wittingly."[1]

Knowing what we now know about the information that Edward Snowden revealed to the media, Clapper's statement is quite controversial. Clapper has since clarified his statement. Although Snowden has not pinpointed an exact moment or specific event that led to his final decision to leak NSA secrets, he did mention Clapper's less than truthful testimony as having been one of the things that motivated him to take action

What Is a Whistleblower?

Many people do not believe that Edward Snowden qualifies as a true whistleblower. A whistleblower is someone who reveals information or actions that they feel might be illegal. During a 2016 press conference, White House press secretary Josh Earnest was asked about Snowden as a whistleblower. Earnest responded, "I don't think it makes sense, because Edward Snowden is not a whistleblower. There actually is a specific process that is well-established and well-protected that allows whistleblowers to raise concerns that they have, particularly when it relates to confidential or classified information, to do so in a way that protects the national security secrets of the United States. That is not what Mr. Snowden did."[2]

about what he knew about NSA secret surveillance of American citizens.[3]

Contacting Glenn Greenwald and Laura Poitras

Before leaving the United States on May 20, 2013, and traveling to Hong Kong to meet with Glenn Greenwald and Laura Poitras, Snowden had to take many careful steps to ensure he could accomplish his illegal task. By March 2013, Snowden had left his job at the computer company Dell and took a new position at Booz Allen Hamilton, a contractor for the NSA.[4] Various interviews with Snowden indicate that he took his job as a systems administrator with Booz Allen Hamilton because the position granted him access to many top-secret files—files Snowden wanted to steal and leak to journalists as evidence of the NSA's mass surveillance activities. In a 2013 interview with the *Washington Post,* Snowden said, "My position with Booz Allen Hamilton granted me access to lists of machines all over the world the NSA hacked."[5]

In April 2013, Snowden and his girlfriend, Lindsay Mills, moved into a new rented home in Hawaii. Snowden only stayed at his new job at Booz Allen Hamilton for a

Snowden reached out to Laura Poitras and Glenn Greenwald to share his revelations about the NSA mass surveillance. It took many attempts to get the documentary filmmaker and journalist to listen.

total of four weeks before leaving. Not even Mills knew what had happened to him when he disappeared.[6]

Many months earlier, in December 2012, Snowden first contacted *Guardian* freelance journalist Glenn Greenwald.[7] After reading many of Greenwald's essays and articles, Snowden concluded that he was the person he wanted to help bring the NSA mass surveillance news to light. Starting in December 2012, Snowden repeatedly tried to communicate with Greenwald to get the ball rolling.

Snowden was paranoid about people around him, and he was worried he was already being monitored. What he was doing was illegal, even though he felt it should be done for the good of US citizens. He would communicate with Greenwald and tell him more only if he could convince him to start using encryption software so they could chat more securely. Encryption software changes information into a code to keep people from being able to read it without a special password. Because Greenwald was busy and because Snowden was vague about the details of his request, the two never connected further beyond those initial email communications.

Snowden did not give up. He went on to contact a close friend and associate of Greenwald's, the documentary filmmaker Laura Poitras. She eventually received an email from Snowden that stated, "I am a senior member of the intelligence community. This won't be a waste of your time."[8] Poitras was familiar with encryption, so they were able to communicate securely. Poitras even gave Snowden her encryption key, which is like an elaborate password that allows encrypted communications to be decoded by the receiver.

Snowden then described one of the thousands of top-secret files he eventually planned on releasing to her. One of them was Presidential Policy Directive 20 a "top-secret 18-page document issued in October 2012. It said that the agency was tapping fibre optic cables, intercepting telephone landing points and bugging on a global scale."[9]

Snowden also told her he wanted Glenn Greenwald involved, too. Poitras and Greenwald eventually met, and she described the collection of mass surveillance that her mysterious source was promising. At the time, Greenwald did not know Poitras's source was the same contact he had chatted briefly with months earlier. Greenwald then approached the *Guardian*'s US editor, Janine Gibson. They talked over the phone about secret NSA documents, but the conversation did not last long and they decided to meet at the *Guardian*'s US office in New York City to talk further.[10] Once in New York, Greenwald was given the go-ahead to meet Snowden in Hong Kong. The *Guardian* also sent along another journalist with many years of experience, Ewen MacAskill.

> "I am a senior member of the intelligence community. This won't be a waste of your time."

Laura Poitras was going to Hong Kong, too, and on the flight to Hong Kong, she shared with Greenwald many thousands of top-secret files she had received from Snowden. Greenwald was so fascinated by what he was reading that he did not sleep at all during the long sixteen-hour flight from New York City to Hong Kong.

Reporter Ewen MacAskill accompanied Glenn Greenwald and Laura Poitras when they first met Edward Snowden in 2013. MacAskill's reporting on Edward Snowden helped his newspaper, the *Guardian*, win the Pulitzer Prize for Public Service in 2014.

The Green Alligator and a Rubik's Cube

The initial meeting between Snowden, Greenwald, and Poitras unfolded like something right out of a Hollywood spy thriller. Snowden had given specific instructions to meet him inside a public area inside the Mira Hotel in Kowloon, Hong Kong, next to a large green plastic alligator. If he did not show up right away, Greenwald and Poitras were instructed to return twenty minutes later and wait again. They were also told to give a code phrase to identify themselves. The last bit of identifying information Snowden gave Greenwald and Poitras was that he'd be holding a Rubik's Cube in his left hand.[11]

The meeting finally took place on Monday, June 3, 2013. Greenwald and Poitras followed Snowden up the elevator to his hotel room—room 1014.[12] Because Snowden was so young, Greenwald was considering that he might be the son of the source he was supposed to meet. He could not imagine someone so young had such high-level clearance with government documents. He even considered that the entire meeting might not be legitimate. Once in the hotel room, Snowden began to disclose who he was, what he had, and what his intentions were. The other reporter from the *Guardian*, Ewen MacAskill, was not at the initial meeting, but after his presence in Hong Kong was explained to Snowden, they eventually met, too. Snowden provided MacAskill with all his identification and credentials as proof of who he was.

As soon as they all realized Snowden was whom he claimed, and what he had to offer was real and not a hoax, MacAskill reported back to his bosses at the *Guardian* in

"I Have Nothing to Hide"

Despite the revelations about NSA mass surveillance, some people think mass surveillance is not something most Americans need to worry about. The argument that is often discussed is that people with nothing to hide should not be worried if the NSA is collecting data on them and millions of other innocent Americans.

A 2016 panel discussion was held at the University of Arizona College of Social and Behavioral Sciences. MIT professor Noam Chomsky, *Guardian* journalist Glenn Greenwald, and Edward Snowden discussed finding a balance between government intrusion and individual rights in a free society.

During the discussion, Snowden said, "Arguing that you don't care about the right to privacy because you have nothing to hide is no different than saying you don't care about free speech because you have nothing to say."[13]

New York. He even contacted the *Guardian* with a code phrase in case communications were being monitored.

"How's the Guinness?" his boss asked. MacAskill was being asked about beer, but the question was really a reference to whether or not Snowden, and what he claimed to have, was genuine.

MacAskill replied, "The Guinness is good."[14]

Over the next few days, Greenwald and MacAskill interviewed Snowden, and Poitras filmed the encounter. The information and documents Snowden disclosed

The Mira Hotel in Kowloon, Hong Kong, was ground zero where Edward Snowden disclosed his identity as the leaker of thousands of top-secret NSA documents revealing mass surveillance.

painted a bleak and frightening picture of the NSA's surveillance capabilities and how that had grown since 9/11. According to Snowden, the NSA had been gobbling up the communications records and metadata of millions of Americans and was storing them indefinitely. The metadata is information that provides even more details about data sets. This gave the government boundless information about innocent Americans.

Snowden also described NSA infrastructure that is automatically ingesting billions of communications from Americans without anyone being specifically targeted. The stored data can then be used at a later date to scan backward into a person's past in an effort to search for specific information. Snowden also explained how the phone in the hotel room, cell phones, laptops, and other connected devices could all have their cameras and microphones accessed by the NSA and used to spy on a person if the NSA decided it wanted to monitor someone.[15]

> "I'll be working on a Rubik's Cube so you can identify me."

Footage shot by Poitras from her award-winning 2014 documentary *Citizenfour* show Snowden covering his head with a pillowcase because he was so paranoid of his password becoming exposed. Snowden also gave the reporters documents revealing how the British intelligence and security agency, Government Communications Headquarters (GCHQ), works closely with the United States and has mass surveillance programs of its own, too. One GCHQ program called Tempora taps into world fiber optic cables and collects and stores emails, social network posts, web histories, and calls. This collected data is then shared with the NSA.[16]

The first news article was written by Glenn Greenwald and was published by the *Guardian* on June 6, 2013. It detailed how a top-secret Foreign Intelligence Surveillance Court (FISC) order allowed the NSA to collect the phone records from millions of Verizon customers within the United States for up to three months. The article also reported how this data collection was happening indiscriminately to millions of Verizon customers, regardless of who they were. The Verizon customers did not need to be under any sort of suspicion of illegal activity. According to the *Guardian* article, "Under the terms of the blanket order, the numbers of both parties on a call are handed over, as is location data, call duration, unique identifiers, and the time and duration of all calls. The contents of the conversation itself are not covered."[17]

This information was just the tip of the iceberg. Greenwald felt that Snowden had revealed so much information he felt it needed to be made into separate stories for the newspaper. More details were sure to be revealed.

CHAPTER FOUR

The News Gets Reported

• • • • • • • • • • • • • •

On June 6, 2013, the *Guardian* published the first article based on Snowden's leaked documents. The article was called "NSA collecting phone records of millions of Verizon customers daily." The news spread very quickly. The following day, June 7, 2013, journalist Barton Gellman and Laura Poitras published another article in the *Washington Post* about a top-secret government program, code-named PRISM. According to the article, "The National Security Agency and the FBI are tapping directly into the central servers of nine leading US Internet companies, extracting audio and video chats, photographs, e-mails, documents, and connection logs that enable analysts to track foreign targets."[1]

The documents Snowden illegally took from the NSA and revealed to journalists caused instant reactions throughout the news media, the United States government, and other governments throughout the world.

United States Responds

Reactions to the NSA leaks from different parts of the United States government happened quickly. As soon as the first *Guardian* article was published, a news conference was quickly held with senators Dianne Feinstein from California and Saxby Chambliss from Georgia. Feinstein defended the NSA's mass collection of information and explained how no actual content of phone conversations was ever recorded. She said that the data collection had been going on for seven years

Glenn Greenwald

Before Glenn Greenwald became known for his reporting on NSA leaker Edward Snowden, he was already very accomplished. Greenwald was born on March 6, 1967, in New York City. He attended George Washington University and studied philosophy. Afterward, he attended New York University School of Law and worked for a law firm before running his own for ten years. In 2005, Greenwald began his own political blog, Unclaimed Territory. Greenwald went on to work for Salon.com, writing columns about civil liberties and privacy. Greenwald also wrote about US intelligence and the CIA. Edward Snowden contacted Greenwald because the thought his articles on civil liberties and US national security were so strong. Greenwald's reporting on Edward Snowden led to the *Washington Post* and the *Guardian* winning the 2014 Pulitzer Prize for public service.

and that the United States Senate was aware of the program. The records could only be obtained under strict circumstances.[2]

Other reactions from other government officials followed. All of them spoke out against Snowden's actions.

- In reference to Snowden, Shawn Turner, a spokesperson for the Office of the Director of National Intelligence, said, "Any person who has a security clearance knows that he or she has an obligation to protect classified information and abide by the law."[3]

- Justice Department spokeswoman Nanda Chitre said, "[The Justice Department] is in the initial stages of an investigation into the unauthorized disclosure of classified information by an individual with authorized access."[4]

- National Security Agency director General Keith Alexander said of the Snowden leaks, "I think it was irreversible and significant damage to this nation."[5]

- President Barack Obama said, "What I can say unequivocally is that if you are a US person, the NSA cannot listen to your telephone calls, and the NSA cannot target your e-mails."[6]

Edward Snowden was aware that he could face harsh backlash for his actions. He had never wanted to keep his identity hidden or secret. He also did not want others he worked with, his family, or his girlfriend, Lindsay Mills,

On January 17, 2014, President Barack Obama spoke about how he revised the powers of the NSA after the Snowden leaks were revealed to the world. While collection of phone data is still permitted, there are new guidelines about how the data is collected and used.

to be examined or scrutinized for what he had done. On Tuesday, June 11, 2013, the *Guardian* published another article called, "Edward Snowden: The Whistleblower Behind the NSA Surveillance Revelations." The article was written by Glenn Greenwald, Ewen MacAskill, and Laura Poitras from Hong Kong, and detailed how Snowden, "a 29-year-old former technical assistant for the CIA and current employee of the defense contractor Booz Allen Hamilton" was the one who leaked the documents. In the article, Snowden was quoted as saying, "I have no intention of hiding who I am because I know I have done nothing wrong."[7]

Although Snowden did not mind taking the blame for what he had done, he also indicated that he did not want the story to be about him. His intention was to release the top-secret NSA documents to journalists and let them and their news organizations make decisions about what should be published and revealed to the public. Snowden also spoke to Glenn Greenwald about his decision to become a whistleblower. He said, "You can't wait around for someone else to act." Snowden also claimed, "The government has granted itself power it is not entitled to. There is no public oversight. The result is people like myself have the latitude to go further than they are allowed to."[8]

Where Is Snowden?

As soon as Snowden's identity was revealed by the media, he disappeared. On June 18, 2013, the deputy director of the FBI, Sean Joyce, testified before the House Intelligence Committee and stated that the recently disclosed PRISM program had helped to stop several terrorist attacks. Panel chairman Mike Rogers also asked National Security Agency director General Keith

"You can't wait around for someone else to act."

Alexander if the NSA could "flip a switch" to monitor Americans various communications. Alexander replied,

On June 12, 2013, when asked if he could tap into any American's phone calls or email, General Keith Alexander, director of the National Security Agency, replied, "I know of no way to do that."

"no." Rogers then asked again to further clarify, "So the technology does not exist for any individual or group of individuals at the NSA to flip a switch to listen to Americans' phone calls or read their e-mails?" Alexander then replied, "That is correct."[9]

On June 21, 2013, federal prosecutors filed a criminal complaint and charged Snowden with espionage and theft of government property. Snowden was officially charged with "unauthorized communication of national defense information" and "willful communication of classified communications intelligence information to an unauthorized person."[10] The United States government also asked Hong Kong to issue an arrest warrant for Snowden with the hope that he would be held there and eventually extradited to, or handed over to, the United States.

Tensions between the United States and other countries began to heat up over the news about unrestricted NSA surveillance. Snowden had become a sort of international hot potato, and a guessing game began about exactly where Snowden was located. By June 23, 2013, the United States government had revoked Snowden's passport, making it no longer valid for travel. However, he had already managed to board an airplane from Hong Kong to Moscow, fleeing in an effort to seek asylum, or political protection, in another country.

On the same day, the Hong Kong government announced that the United States' request for Snowden's extradition did not "fully comply with the legal requirements under Hong Kong law." This confusion and extra paperwork between Hong Kong and the

United States permitted Snowden to exit the country with ease.[11]

According to a BBC news article, China's official news agency, called Xinhua, said that the news that Snowden revealed showed "clearly troubling signs" from the United States. "They demonstrate that the United States, which has long been trying to play innocent as a victim of cyber attacks, has turned out to be the biggest villain in our age."[12]

The Chinese state news organization also stated, "It owes too an explanation to China and other countries it has allegedly spied on. It has to share with the world

Laura Poitras

Documentary filmmaker Laura Poitras was born in Boston, Massachusetts, on February 2, 1964. After high school, Poitras moved to San Francisco, where she worked as a chef. She then studied filmmaking at the San Francisco Art Institute. She moved to New York City in 1992 and studied documentary filmmaking at the New School for Social Research. Poitras is a journalist and filmmaker known for her 2014 NSA documentary, *Citizenfour*, part of which came from footage she shot when she first met Edward Snowden in 2013. *Citizenfour* was the third film in Poitras's trilogy on the changes in America after the terrorist attacks of September 11, 2001, which also included *The Oath* (2010) and *My Country, My Country* (2006). Poitras shared the 2014 Pulitzer Prize for Public Service for her work on reporting about the NSA.

the range, extent and intent of its clandestine hacking programs."[13]

Landing in Russia

Once Snowden landed in Moscow, Russia, his plan was to continue onward to Cuba and eventually fly to Ecuador, where he was hoping to find asylum. On June 25, 2013, Russian president Vladimir Putin held a news conference and ended the mystery of Snowden's whereabouts. Putin confirmed that Snowden was in the

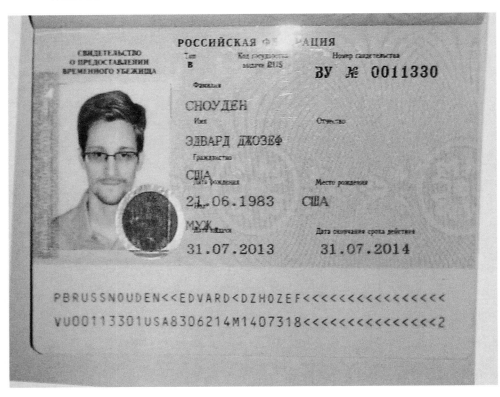

Snowden spent several weeks living at Sheremetyevo International Airport in Moscow, Russia. Eventually he was granted asylum in Russia that has been extended until 2020. He was granted refugee documents by Russia to show his temporary status.

"transit area" of the Sheremetyevo International Airport, an area between the arrival gates and Russia's passport control checkpoint. This area is an international zone within the airport. Putin also added, "The sooner he selects his final destination point, the better both for us and for himself."[14] Despite Putin's refusal to extradite Snowden to the United States, he still indicated Snowden was a free man and expressed his desire for him to continue onward to another country. Putin, like the leaders in Hong Kong, did not seem to want Snowden to remain in the country.

President Barack Obama spoke at a news conference in Dakar, Senegal, on June 27, 2013. During the conference, he was asked about Edward Snowden. Obama said he had not made a personal call to Russian president Vladimir Putin or previously to the Chinese president, Xi Jinping, about the extradition of Edward Snowden because he felt it was unnecessary. Obama felt it was within the jurisdiction of law enforcement and not serious enough to require his involvement. He tried to downplay the incident by saying, "No, I'm not going to be scrambling jets to get a 29-year-old hacker."[15]

> "No I'm not going to be scrambling jets to get a 29-year-old hacker."

With his passport revoked, Snowden was unable to leave Russia. He continued to explore the option of possibly seeking asylum in Ecuador and also flying to Cuba. The US government issued statements to many countries that

Snowden was attempting to seek asylum in, warning the countries to hand him over if he arrived at their borders.

According to the founder of WikiLeaks, an organization that reveals classified information, Snowden had applied for asylum in as many as twenty countries, including, France, Germany, Ireland, China, Cuba, Ecuador, Iceland and elsewhere.[16] By late June the president of Ecuador, Rafael Correa, announced that US vice president Joe Biden asked him to deny Snowden asylum. Correa explained that the decision was his to make, as the president of Ecuador, but he could not decide or reveal what he would do unless Snowden was actually in Ecuador.[17]

On June 30, 2013, Snowden applied for asylum in Russia at the consular office of Moscow's Sheremetyevo airport. This news prompted a statement from Russian president Vladimir Putin. He stated about Snowden, "If he wants to go somewhere and someone will take him, go ahead. If he wants to stay here, there is one condition— he must stop his work aimed at bringing harm to our American partners, as strange as that sounds coming from my mouth."[18]

By late July 2013, Edward Snowden was still living at the Moscow airport. By August 1, Snowden had left the airport for the first time after he was granted temporary asylum in Russia. As of 2017, Edward Snowden is still living within Russia and his asylum status there has been extended until 2020.

CHAPTER FIVE

Many Questions, Many Reactions

• •

In the months that followed Snowden's leaked NSA files, many news reports slowly cropped up. The NSA, which is known for its intense secrecy, was suddenly very exposed and was being examined by the entire world. As the huge number of documents Snowden leaked were being carefully examined by journalists and media experts, details of alleged NSA spying and surveillance were slowly exposed. The top-secret documents showed that the NSA's surveillance targeted foreign countries, American allies, businesses, foreign citizens, as well as suspected terrorists—over 1,000 targets in all.[1] The revelations continued, as did the mounting questions. Exactly how many documents did Edward Snowden steal? What news was coming next? And how could this breach of security happen to the most secretive intelligence agency in the world? The answers slowly started to trickle in.

Unable to travel freely since being granted asylum in Russia, Snowden has since appeared via video feed around the world. This screen shot of Edward Snowden was reportedly shot on October 9, 2013. It was taken from AFPTV footage at an unidentified location.

● ●

How Many Documents Were Leaked?

The question of exactly how many documents Edward Snowden took from the NSA is not an easy one to answer. Initially, Glenn Greenwald reported that Snowden had given Laura Poitras between 9,000 and 10,000 top-secret documents.[2] Later, reports from National Security Agency director, Keith Alexander, estimated the amount of stolen NSA documents to be around 200,000.[3] The figure continued to grow. Many reports were inconsistent, and it was hard to get the public a definitive answer. One article in the *Daily Beast* quoted someone who had previously worked as a US counterintelligence officer, "[I] think Snowden has been planning this for years and has stashed files all over the Internet."[4] In another interview, Glenn Greenwald explained to the *Daily Beast* that Snowden had taken steps to insure his personal security by making sure more files would become available if anything happened to him.

By December 2013, the NSA had disclosed to CBS's *60 Minutes* that they believed Snowden had stolen 1.7 million documents and that he provided journalists with about 200,000 of them. The NSA also revealed that they believed Snowden still had access to an additional 1.5 million documents.[5]

Nearly one year after the initial Snowden leak, the director of national intelligence, James Clapper, revealed, "It doesn't look like he took as much" as the NSA first estimated. "We're still investigating, but we think that a lot of what he looked at, he couldn't pull down. . .Some things we thought he got he apparently didn't."[6]

Snowden himself had initially stated he had turned over all the files he had to Greenwald and Poitras in Hong Kong, and that he had taken no classified files with him to Russia. Discrepancies and inconsistencies in Snowden's claims soon began to surface. In an interview with the *South China Morning Post* from June 12, 2013—just two days after Snowden left Greenwald and Poitras—he revealed that he had access to more files and intended to eventually leak them. Even if Snowden did not have more files in his possession, he made it clear that he had access to them somewhere. Glenn Greenwald confirmed this during an interview he had with the Associated Press.

Other Famous Whistleblowers

Edward Snowden may have perpetrated the largest leak of classified information in US history, but he is not the first whistleblower to leak secrets.

- In 1971, police officer Frank Serpico testified to the Knapp Commission exposing corruption within the New York City Police Department. Serpico was the first officer to do so.[7]

- Jeffrey Wigand was a scientist who worked for the tobacco company Brown & Williamson as vice president of research. In 1994, Wigand broke a confidentiality agreement after he exposed thousands of tobacco industry documents detailing that cigarettes were an addictive device for the delivery of nicotine into the human body.[8]

- Bradley Manning was a US Army intelligence analyst who leaked hundreds of thousands of classified files to the organization that discloses secret information and news leaks, WikiLeaks. In 2013, Manning was sentenced to thirty-five years in prison for espionage. Manning is a transgender woman and became legally recognized as Chelsea Elizabeth Manning in 2014. On January 17, 2017, President Barack Obama commuted, or reduced, most of Manning's remaining prison sentence, allowing release in May 2017.[9]

He said Snowden "is in possession of literally thousands of documents."[10]

Although the release of Snowden documents has slowed in recent years, no one truly knows exactly how many more might exist or if more revelations are yet to come.

Embarrassing News Keeps Coming

Snowden's leaked files revealed that the NSA and the British intelligence organization Government Communications Headquarters (GCHQ) directed their surveillance at more than 1,000 targets, countries, and world leaders globally.[11] The real surprise to everyone

Army intelligence analyst Chelsea Manning was sentenced to thirty-five years in prison for releasing thousands of classified documents, battlefield reports, and videos. The sentence was later commuted to just seven years, and Manning was released in 2017.

came after it was learned from the leaked Snowden documents that many of the targets were not just terrorists and enemy states but also close allies of the United States. According to one confidential memo, the NSA monitored the calls of thirty-five world leaders.[12] More leaked Snowden documents did not help the situation, which caused some political tensions for the White House and President Barack Obama.

On October 21, 2013, the French newspaper *Le Monde* published an article that alleged the NSA had been "monitoring and tapping" the telephone calls and text messages of millions of French citizens—as many as 70 million in one thirty-day span in 2012. President Barack Obama called French president François Hollande to address the issue. A White House readout of the call was released to the press on October 21, 2013: "The President spoke today with President Hollande of France. The United States and France are allies and friends, and share a close working relationship on a wide range of issues, including security and intelligence. The President and President Hollande discussed recent disclosures in the press—some of which have distorted our activities and some of which raise legitimate questions for our friends and allies about how these capabilities are employed. The President made clear that the United States has begun to review the way that we gather intelligence, so that we properly balance the legitimate security concerns of our citizens and allies with the privacy concerns that all people share. The two Presidents agreed that we should continue to discuss these issues in diplomatic channels moving forward."[13]

Several days later, on October 23, 2013, German chancellor Angela Merkel called President Obama after she learned of news from the German periodical *Der Spiegel* that the NSA might have been monitoring her personal phone. This news was reported based on a leaked Snowden file. Merkel reportedly expressed her disapproval if the allegations turned out to be true.

During a White House press conference on October 25, 2013, Jim Sciutto, a reporter from CNN, asked about the alleged tapping of Chancellor Merkel's phone. White House press secretary Jay Carney responded, "I can tell you that the president assured the chancellor that the

Despite uncomfortable allegations that the NSA may have been monitoring German chancellor Angela Merkel's personal phone, relations between Germany and the United States remained strong.

United States is not monitoring, and will not monitor the communications of the chancellor. The United States greatly values our close cooperation with Germany on a broad range of shared security challenges."[14]

How Did Snowden Do It?

It was not long before the question of exactly how Edward Snowden managed to make off with possibly 1.7 million highly classified or top-secret files began to get asked. By his own admission, Snowden said he was

Deep Throat and Watergate

Scandal is not new to the United States government. On June 17, 1972, several people were arrested after a break-in at the Democratic National Committee office inside the Watergate office-apartment-hotel complex in Washington, DC. Investigative journalists Bob Woodward and Carl Bernstein of the *Washington Post* uncovered information that showed that President Richard Nixon attempted to cover up the break-in because of his administration's connection to it. Throughout their reporting, Woodward and Bernstein were provided information from a secret source known as "Deep Throat." Woodward and Bernstein eventually won the Pulitzer Prize for their reporting on the scandal. As a result of President Nixon's involvement in the Watergate scandal, he was forced to resign in August 1974. In 2005, FBI associate William Mark Felt admitted he was the informant known as Deep Throat. [15]

intimately familiar with NSA practices, protocols, and security measures. He also said that he took a pay cut from his job at Dell to work for Booz Allen Hamilton in order to gain access to the files he wished to leak. Before disappearing from China and reappearing

> **"I can tell you that the president assured the chancellor that the United States is not monitoring, and will not monitor the communications of the chancellor."**

in Russia, Snowden told the *South China Morning Post*, "My position with Booz Allen Hamilton granted me access to lists of machines all over the world the NSA hacked. . .That is why I accepted that position about three months ago." Snowden also said, "Booz was not the most I've been paid."[16]

Other reports surfaced that named the outdated NSA technology as one of the reasons for Snowden's ease in making off with so many documents. According to an intelligence official who spoke to NBC News, "It's 2013 and the NSA is stuck in 2003 technology."[17]

There was also a warning about Snowden. It came back in 2009 when he was working for the CIA and his superiors realized he had attempted to access unauthorized files. According to an article in the *New York Times*, "his supervisor wrote a derogatory report in his personnel file, noting a distinct change in the young man's behavior and work habits, as well as a troubling suspicion." The warning sign was there, but it did not follow him onward to the NSA.[18]

A friend of Snowden's, Mavanee Anderson, wrote an article for the *Times Free Press* on June 12, 2013. In the personal article on Snowden, whom she called Ed, she revealed that, "At the time when we were in close contact—from the summer of 2007 through the first part of 2009—he was already experiencing a crisis of conscience of sorts." Snowden was working for the CIA during this period.[19]

> **"At the time when we were in close contact . . . he was already experiencing a crisis of conscience of sorts."**

Today, many of the documents Snowden leaked can be accessed online by anyone. On March 4, 2015, the *Canadian Journalists for Free Expression* (CJFE) launched the Snowden Digital Surveillance Archive online. The archive contains only documents that were released by Snowden to journalists and eventually published by various news media organizations online. The archive contains about four hundred documents and is only a small portion of what Snowden is said to have taken from the NSA. Another nonprofit civil liberties organization, the Electronic Frontier Foundation, has also created an online database of all the leaked Snowden files, NSA Primary Sources, which were published by various news media organizations.

CHAPTER SIX

Hero or Traitor?

Is Edward Snowden a hero for exposing NSA mass surveillance on Americans, or is he a traitor for illegally uncovering security secrets that help keep Americans safe and secure? Many news media outlets have posed this question in countless articles, essays, and opinion pieces. There are many strong words of condemnation, as well as high praise for Snowden from many different sources. Even among politicians and government officials there has been disagreement. While many, even including President Barack Obama, talked about reform and review of the NSA, the issue of Snowden's actions is almost always considered separately from what he leaked.

Snowden—Hero to the United States

Praise for Edward Snowden as a hero is not hard to come by. Snowden himself wrote a short article for the German periodical *Der Spiegel* on November 1, 2013. In the article, he justified his actions by explaining how they resulted in "increased oversight and new legislation." Snowden also claimed, "Citizens have to fight suppression of information on matters of vital public importance. To tell the truth is not a crime."[1]

The human rights group Amnesty International ran a campaign for Edward Snowden's pardon, praising his actions and labeling him a hero. According to the Amnesty International website, "Edward Snowden is a hero not a traitor. He stood up for our rights, prompting a global debate on mass surveillance that changed the world—yet he faces decades in prison for it."[2] The website allows for visitors to add their name, email, and country to a petition for Snowden's pardon.

> "To tell the truth is not a crime."

An opinion piece written by Philip Giraldi and published for the *American Conservative* on July 16, 2013, argued that Snowden is a whistleblower and not a traitor. In the article, Giraldi argues that the charge of treason against Snowden is debatable and would not hold up since Snowden did not seek to aid any enemies of the United States. The article states that Snowden "has revealed only one actual secret that matters, which is the United States government's serial violation of the Fourth Amendment to the Constitution through its collection of personal information on millions of innocent American citizens without any probable cause or search warrant."[3]

A "Hero" portrait of Edward Snowden was displayed during a protest against government surveillance in October 2013, in Washington, DC. The stark graphic image is similar to the Barack Obama "Hope" poster on display during Obama's 2008 presidential campaign.

During a Democratic presidential debate in 2015, some candidates defended Snowden. Former Rhode Island governor Lincoln Chafee praised Snowden's actions and said, "What Snowden did showed that the American government was acting illegally for the Fourth Amendment. So, I would bring him home." During the same debate, Senator Bernie Sanders of Vermont was asked if he would shut down the NSA surveillance program. Sanders replied, "Absolutely. Of course."[4]

Douglas Rushkoff reported for CNN with a clear opinion that Snowden is a hero. In his article from June 10, 2013, Rushkoff recalled Daniel Ellsberg, an intelligence contractor who exposed classified documents about the Vietnam War to the *New York Times* in 1971. Rushkoff compared Snowden to Ellsberg and recalled how the public eventually decided Ellsberg was a hero. Rushkoff explained, "You'd think we would be even more outraged by what he [Snowden] uncovered than we were by the surveillance of Ellsberg. After all, it's not just one lone loose cannon being wiretapped here, it's all of us being monitored. Snowden has not uncovered a human conspiracy here but the workings of the machine itself. And it's a machine that really does require some human intervention." Rushkoff concludes his opinion piece for CNN thankful that people like Snowden exist who are not robots and can act with conscience.[5]

On January 1, 2014, the *New York Times* published an opinion article called "Edward Snowden, Whistle-Blower." The article argues that Snowden is a true whistleblower for exposing important violations that the government was taking part in. A few of the violations Snowden exposed included the breaking of federal laws, breaking into data centers around the world, and undermining of internet encryption systems. The violations also included the violation of the Fourth Amendment of the Constitution and the fact that the director of national intelligence, James Clapper, lied to Congress regarding the NSA's surveillance of the

Protests Supporting Snowden

Soon after Edward Snowden's identity was first reveled by the *Guardian* in 2013, protests occurred worldwide in favor of his actions, including in New York and Hong Kong.

The "Stop Watching Us" protest in Washington, DC, was held on Saturday, October 26, 2013. The protest was against mass surveillance by the NSA, and thousands of people attended. According to the *Guardian,* the rally was organized by diverse groups, including "an unusually broad coalition of left- and right-wing groups, including everything from the American Civil Liberties Union, the Green Party, Color of Change and Daily Kos to the Libertarian Party, FreedomWorks and Young Americans for Liberty." Many protestors held up "Thank you, Edward Snowden" signs to show their support for the man who had only recently become known to the world.[6]

American public. The article concluded that anyone who reveals so many illegal government violations should not face a prison sentence.[7]

Despite all the praise and admiration Snowden has received, there are many who feel exactly the opposite about what Snowden did.

Snowden—Traitor to the United States

While some writers and journalists simply questioned whether Edward Snowden was a traitor to his country, others were surer in their conviction that he was a traitor and was guilty of treason. Some even speculated that Snowden might be a spy for a foreign power.

An article in the *Diplomat* by Zachary Keck from December 21, 2013, called "Yes, Edward Snowden Is a Traitor" separates Snowden's disclosures from his actions. Keck expressed how the NSA surveillance Snowden disclosed is not the issue, but rather how Snowden went about disclosing it. Keck explained his position in the article and pointed to Snowden fleeing the United States to Hong Kong rather than staying in the United States to face justice. According to Keck, "Snowden's flight to Hong Kong and then Moscow showed he wasn't willing to suffer the consequences for his actions, calling into question how much he believed in his cause." Keck continued with his claim that Snowden is a traitor and pointed to the careless manner in which he disclosed information. Rather than take a few documents, Snowden "collected an apparently unknowable amount of information (unknowable to both him and the NSA) and dumped it on the doorsteps of largely foreign newspapers." Keck concluded by stating that Snowden's actions undermined US alliances and aided US adversaries.[8]

An article in the *Telegraph* by Charles Moore published July 5, 2013, argued Snowden's guilt as well. At the time, Snowden was still living in the Moscow airport before Russia had granted him temporary asylum. Moore claimed that Snowden was seeking asylum in other countries because of the United States human rights violations he exposed. According to the article, "Now let him [Snowden] find out how hollow those rights are

Edward Snowden became a symbol against government spying in the months and years after he leaked classified NSA documents. Posters thanking Edward Snowden for his sacrifice were held up during a protest outside of the US Capitol.

when not guaranteed within a democratic legal order. Let him eat the free peanuts in the transit lounge of life, and learn, too late, what is needed to defend a free people." Moore concluded by stating, "There is a heresy about the web, which is that it emancipates its user from his duty to his neighbor and his country. In reality, it is the product of free countries, not a replacement for them. Edward Snowden is a devotee of this false doctrine, not a martyr for the truth."[9]

A *Wall Street Journal* opinion video from September 16, 2016, featured an interview by Mary Kissel with

World Day Against Cyber Censorship

The World Day Against Cyber Censorship is an online rally held each year on March 12 to support free speech and protest censorship. In 2016, the internet browser company AdBlock used its browser service, which is designed to block advertisements, and replaced the ads with new public service announcement protesting censorship.[10] AdBlock partnered with the human rights group Amnesty International, Edward Snowden, the controversial Russian rock band Pussy Riot, and Chinese artist Ai Weiwei for the campaign that featured web banners and images with quotes from them.

Edward Snowden's quote for his AdBlock banner read: "Even if you're not doing anything wrong, you're being watched and recorded."[11]

University of California, Berkeley, law professor John Yoo about why Edward Snowden should not be granted a presidential pardon. Yoo argued that Snowden's revelations did not disclose illegal activity because all were approved by Congress and supported by United States courts. Yoo concluded by expressing his belief that if Snowden believed what he did was right, he should return to the United States to face justice here.[12]

The House Intelligence Committee Report

The most compelling evidence against Edward Snowden eventually came from some members of the House Permanent Select Committee on Intelligence. The bipartisan House Intelligence Committee report is called "Executive Summary of Review of the Unauthorized Disclosures of Former National Security Agency Contractor Edward Snowden." The full report was classified, but a declassified portion was released to the media and the public. The three-page report begins by stating: "The Committee remains hopeful that Snowden will return to the United States to face justice."

> **"Even if you're not doing anything wrong, you're being watched and recorded."**

The following points come from a section of the report released to the public:

- First, Snowden caused tremendous damage to national security, and the vast majority of the documents he stole have nothing to do with programs impacting individual privacy interests—they instead pertain to military, defense, and intelligence programs of great interest to America's adversaries.

- Second, Snowden was not a whistleblower.

- Third, two weeks before Snowden began mass downloads of classified documents, he was reprimanded after engaging in a workplace spat with NSA managers.

- Fourth, Snowden was, and remains, a serial exaggerator and fabricator.

- Finally, the Committee remains concerned that more than three years after the start of the unauthorized disclosures, NSA, and the IC as a whole, have not done enough to minimize the risk of another massive unauthorized disclosure.[13]

The entire declassified portion of the summary can be found on the website of the House Permanent Select Committee on Intelligence.

CHAPTER SEVEN

The Snowden Effect

• • • • • • • •

The reactions to Edward Snowden's leaked NSA documents about mass surveillance earned their own term—the Snowden Effect. Nations, government agencies, technology companies, and even individuals have all reacted in some form or another to the news of mass surveillance spying programs conducted by the NSA. Nations have ended relationships with corporations and altered policies because of what was learned. As a result, the US government reviewed its policies and tightened security. Technology companies have embraced encryption and covet their data now more than ever before. And individuals have also begun to choose companies, technologies, and data protection software all because of the ripple effect caused by Snowden's disclosures.

Government Changes

No one likes to be spied on, but when you learn that your friends are spying on you, the reactions can get even more uncomfortable. When Germany learned in 2013 through documents leaked by Edward Snowden that the NSA might have tapped Chancellor Angela Merkel's personal cellphone, the reaction was swift. Chancellor Merkel was quick to call President Barack Obama, who had to give assurances that her phone was not being tapped. The assurances may have not been enough, because in the months that followed, the German government attempted to negotiate a no-spy deal with the United States. The German government hoped to enter into an intelligence arrangement with the US similar to the agreement between the United States and Britain. The United States, Britain, Canada, Australia, and New Zealand reportedly disclose most intelligence with each other and are often referred to as the Five Eyes. Susan E. Rice, President Obama's national security adviser, had indicated that no such no-spying agreement exists between the US and its allies.

Talks between Germany and the United States regarding a possible agreement stalled just before Chancellor Merkel's visit to the United States in May 2014. The US would not agree to a no-spy agreement with Germany. In the months that followed, Germany became increasingly frustrated with the United States.[1]

By late June 2014, the German government announced it would be canceling a communications contract with the American telecommunications company Verizon. This was prompted by the first news article by the *Guardian* based on leaks by Edward Snowden, revealing that Verizon was collecting the phone records of millions of its customers. According

The first *Guardian* report disclosed that US telecommunications company Verizon collected the phone records from millions of Verizon customers within the United States. Germany soon announced it would cancel a contract with Verizon.

● ●

to a statement in the *New York Times* by Detlef Eppig, managing director of Verizon Germany, "We have made it clear that the US government cannot access customer information that is stored outside the United States."[2]

United States attorney general Eric H. Holder Jr. also gave Germany assurances, but without a formal agreement, Germany was reluctant to take the US at its word. By November 2014, Germany signed a no-spy agreement with Canadian telecommunications company BlackBerry. The company disclosed to Germany that it would not provide confidential data to governments.[3]

Years later, on February 16, 2017, Chancellor Angela Merkel testified before a committee at the German federal parliament about allegations of surveillance in Germany by the NSA. The investigation was a direct result of documents disclosing mass surveillance revealed by Edward Snowden in 2013. Merkel testified, "My standard was that spying among friends is not acceptable, and if it happens we have to intervene."[4]

Despite the tensions, the United States and Germany remain allies and continue to cooperate. Merkel continues to reiterate her statement from 2013 that "spying among friends" is not acceptable.[5]

Corporate Changes

With the news that the NSA was possibly accessing servers of technology companies such as Apple, Google,

The Freedom Act

One of the biggest changes that occurred in the United States after Edward Snowden's leaked NSA documents was the passage of the Freedom Act. The act reauthorized different parts of the Patriot Act, which was passed after the terrorist attacks that took place on September 11, 2001. The purpose of the new bill was to improve the overall structure of the Patriot Act to increase civil liberties for American citizens. One of the most notable improvements is the end of bulk collection of data. This would help ease people's new distrust of the US government and also prevent the government from overreaching its authority on data collection.

and Facebook—or perhaps, even worse, partnering with them—moves towards greater protection of users' privacy were taken. Increased encryption methods as well as new technology have been put in place since Edward Snowden's disclosures. Google posted an announcement on March 20, 2014, on the official Google blog related to security along with advice for creating secure passwords.

> "My standard was that spying among friends is not acceptable."

In September 2014, Apple and Google both announced their new operating systems would be coded or encrypted. Encryption of data makes it difficult to read or decode, even if intercepted by law enforcement. Apple's statement read, in part: "Unlike our competitors, Apple cannot bypass your passcode and therefore cannot access this data. So it's not technically feasible for us to respond to government warrants for the extraction of this data from devices in their possession running iOS 8."[6] According to Apple, breaking the code could take "more than 5 1/2 years to try all combinations of a six-character alphanumeric passcode with lowercase letters and numbers."[7]

Google also announced in September 2014 that its popular Android operating system for smartphones would be encrypted by default. It would take several years for the technology to become available in most of their devices, but it remained dedicated to providing customers with the encryption technologies that would keep its customers safe on the web.[8]

Reactions to New Encryption

The news of Google and Apple device encryption did not sit well with the director of the FBI, James Comey. On September 25, 2014, Comey said in a news conference, "What concerns me about this is companies marketing something expressly to allow people to hold themselves beyond the law."[9] Comey also referred to terrorism and kidnapping cases where law enforcement's access to cellphones could help save lives.

How Do I Protect My Privacy?

Privacy protection for big companies like Apple, Google, and Microsoft is not difficult to implement, yet they still often get hacked. Hackers steal passwords, credit cards, and the identities of internet users. You might wonder what you can do to protect your data, information, and content. A few simple steps can help to keep you secure on the internet at the various websites you visit.

- Use a strong alphanumeric password that uses upper and lowercase letters, numbers, and symbols.

- Use a different password for each website. That way a hacker who gets your password will not be able to use it in other places as well.

- Use two-step verification whenever possible. This is a notification to your mobile device with a special second temporary password for logging in. This extra step can only be accomplished with your mobile phone present, even if someone else has your password.

On December 2, 2015, fourteen people were killed in San Bernardino, California. When the FBI requested Apple's help in unlocking the iPhone of one of the alleged perpetrators, Apple refused.

On February 16, 2016, Apple CEO Tim Cook released a letter to Apple customers stating that Apple has complied with all requests by the FBI

"What concerns me about this is companies marketing something expressly to allow people to hold themselves beyond the law."

that they were legally obligated to assist in. Cook opened the letter by stating, "The United States government has demanded that Apple take an unprecedented step which threatens the security of our customers. We oppose this order, which has implications far beyond the legal case at hand. This moment calls for public discussion, and we want our customers and people around the country to understand what is at stake."

The letter from Cook concluded: "While we believe the FBI's intentions are good, it would be wrong for the government to force us to build a backdoor into our products. And ultimately, we fear that this demand would undermine the very freedoms and liberty our government is meant to protect."[10]

Mark Zuckerberg, CEO of the social network Facebook, personally responded to news of the alleged NSA surveillance program PRISM by posting a statement directly on his Facebook page: "Facebook is not and has never been part of any program to give the US or any

Lawyers, executives, and scientists testified at a House Energy and Commerce subcommittee hearing in Washington, DC, in 2016. The goal is to strike the right balance between privacy and security for American citizens.

• •

other government direct access to our servers. We have never received a blanket request or court order from any government agency asking for information or metadata in bulk, like the one Verizon reportedly received. And if we did, we would fight it aggressively. We hadn't even heard of PRISM before yesterday."[11]

The tug of war between authorities and technology communications companies continues today. The information Edward Snowden exposed is still being debated and reacted to, and new attempts are still being made to avoid government intrusion into our private devices and communications.

CHAPTER EIGHT

Exile in Russia

• •

Since Edward Snowden first found himself in Russia in 2013 while attempting to find asylum in Latin America, he has been unable or unwilling to leave. After spending a short time in the public "transit area" of the Sheremetyevo International Airport in Moscow, Snowden was granted temporary asylum in Russia, allowing him to leave the airport and live on Russian soil. The temporary asylum was eventually extended until 2020.

Since 2013, Snowden has begun a new life in Russia, and even his girlfriend, Lindsay Mills, moved there to live with him in July 2014. Although Snowden's life has changed considerably, his story is still not over, especially since the United States government would like Snowden to return to face espionage charges.

Snowden Lectures from Russia

On June 11, 2013, several days before the United States government charged Edward Snowden with theft, he was fired from his employer Booz Allen Hamilton. According to CNN, Booz Allen Hamilton released a statement at the time, "News reports that this individual has claimed to have leaked classified information are shocking, and if accurate, this action represents a grave violation of the code of conduct and core values of our firm."[1]

Without a job and a source of income, Snowden suddenly needed a new source of income to help support himself in Russia. On October 31, 2013, Snowden's lawyer, Anatoly Kucherena, reported to the news organization Sputnik that Snowden was working for one of Russia's biggest websites doing web maintenance work. His job there was set to start on November 1, 2013. The name of the website was not revealed.[2]

On December 23, 2013, the *Washington Post* published an interview between reporter Barton Gellman and Edward Snowden. Barton reported that Snowden had "turned down millions of dollars in TV and film and book offers." The article described Snowden living simply in Russia, eating ramen noodles and potato chips. In the interview with Gellman, Snowden said, "It has always been really difficult to get me to leave the house . . . I just don't have a lot of needs . . . Occasionally there's things to go do, things to go see, people to meet, tasks to accomplish. But it's really got to be goal-oriented, you know. Otherwise, as long as I can sit down and think and write and talk to somebody, that's more meaningful to me than going out and looking at landmarks."[3]

Eventually though, Snowden began accepting speaking engagements to get his message out to the

After being granted temporary asylum in Russia, Edward Snowden began a new career speaking out against mass surveillance. In 2014, he addressed a packed house at South by Southwest (SXSW) in Austin, Texas, via video feed.

• •

world and was able earn money while doing it. One of his first appearances was at the South by Southwest (SXSW) Conference and Festivals on March 10, 2014, in Austin, Texas. According to the website, the festival celebrates interactive technologies of both the film and music industries. Snowden talked on a live video feed from Russia for an hour. During the conference, he covered various topics such as how individuals and corporations can increase internet security. He also spoke out to defend his actions and stand by the leaking of sensitive NSA information to the press. He also rejected any accusations that the files he took had been somehow acquired by China or Russia. According to an article about the conference on the *Honolulu Star Advertiser*, Snowden was quoted as saying, "I took an oath to support the Constitution, and I felt the Constitution was violated on a massive scale."[4]

Snowden has continued to book himself for numerous teleconference speaking engagements, live-streamed from his location in Russia. By 2015, the fees Snowden received for speaking grew as high as $10,000 for a single appearance.[5] According to Snowden's lawyer, who spoke to the *New York Times*, "His life is very, very rich and full. . . What a remarkable public citizen he's become. How fitting that he has been able to use technology to defeat exile and participate in the debate he started."[6]

Snowden's new career—speaking out about internet security, civil liberties, NSA surveillance, and government reforms—has only continued to grow. According to an online Yahoo! News article from August 2016, "In the last five months, a larger-than-life Snowden

> "I took an oath to support the Constitution, and I felt the Constitution was violated on a massive scale."

has appeared on giant screens to a sold-out audience at the Brooklyn Academy of Music, northern Europe's largest music festival, a symposium on surveillance and civil rights in Tokyo, and Comic Con in San Diego."[7]

Throughout 2015, it was estimated that Snowden earned as much as $200,000 from his speaking engagements.[8] As his popularity increased, so did the cost of his speaking fees. By 2016, Snowden was earning a base price of $25,000 for a video speaking engagement. On February 1, 2017, Edward Snowden spoke via videoconference at the University of Pittsburgh.[9] The event details were listed on the Facebook PCC (Pitt Program Council) event page and the 450 free tickets that were made available for students to attend the event

Asylum and Extradition

When discussing the consequences of Edward Snowden's actions, the words "asylum" and "extradition" often come up. It's important to know the difference between these two words. Asylum is the protection another country offers groups or individuals that arrive there. People leave their homes, regions, or countries for many reasons. War, religious freedom, political turmoil, and in Snowden's case, whistleblowing on alleged illegal activity by the NSA are all reasons people seek asylum.

When a person or group commits a crime and flees to another country, extradition is the process of one government formally requesting the return of that person or group. Countries have different extradition agreements with each other. The United States and Russia have no extradition agreement, therefore President Vladimir Putin was under no formal obligation to send Edward Snowden back to the United States to stand trial for his alleged crimes.

were quickly snapped up. PCC did not disclose how much Snowden was paid for the event.[10] Council spokesperson Joe Miksch said, "The University of Pittsburgh considers free speech and the free exchange of ideas vital tools to educate and enlighten, especially when the speaker or the topic at hand are potentially divisive. The University encourages civil discussion of ideas and viewpoints, and considers the support of that process a distinctive characteristic of the University experience."[11]

A More Secure Internet

On February 2014, Edward Snowden joined the board of the nonprofit Freedom of the Press Foundation, located in San Francisco, California. He has been working with the organization to help reporters communicate securely with their sources. One piece of software being developed is called Sunder. The idea behind the software is the encryption of documents that can only be accessed when several reporters all combine their passwords together. This clever idea insures no one person can be forced to access encrypted files.

The Freedom of the Press Foundation website refers to the famous Watergate scandal as well as the Pentagon papers incident. The foundation's mission is stated as: "dedicated to helping support and defend public-interest journalism focused on exposing mismanagement, corruption, and law-breaking in government. We work to preserve and strengthen the rights guaranteed to the press under the First Amendment through crowdfunding, digital security and internet advocacy."[12]

Scandals are not new for Washington, DC. In 1974, President Richard Nixon resigned from office following revelations disclosed by two *Washington Post* reporters about his administration's role in attempting to cover up the Watergate scandal.

· ·

The Freedom of the Press Foundation website also has three "open-source digital security tools to protect journalists and whistleblowers." The first one is called SecureDrop, which is a free system for whistleblowers to use to submit anonymous documents and information. It is used by more than three dozen news outlets around the world so they can keep their sources safe and secure when sharing information. The second tool is called Secure the News. It tracks the encryption of information by news organization and protects the privacy of readers and journalists. It can also be used to prevent censorship. An encrypted text messaging system called Signal was also developed for use by both journalists and whistleblowers to keep their communications secure.[13]

Snowden Tweets

At 12:00 p.m. on September 29, 2015 Edward Snowden opened a Twitter account. Twitter is an international text-based social network, which has allowed Snowden to continually reach the world whenever he wishes.

Pardon or No Pardon for Snowden?

Before President Barack Obama left office in early 2017, many people and groups were hopeful that he would pardon Edward Snowden and allow him to return to the United States a free man. The presidential pardon power gives the right to the president of the United States to excuse an individual of a crime he or she was convicted for, as well as freeing individuals from prison even before serving out their full sentence.

One group, the US House of Representatives Permanent Select Committee on Foreign Intelligence, hoped that the president would not pardon Snowden. They sent the president a letter on September 15, 2016, urging that he not use his presidential powers to excuse Snowden for his controversial actions.[14] Although President Obama pardoned 212 people during his presidency, Edward Snowden was not one of them.[15]

Snowden's very first tweet was, "Can you hear me now?" which was an advertising tag line for Verizon Wireless to tout the reliability of its network and services. His tweet immediately brought to mind the controversy over the NSA's tapping of Verizon customers

"**Can you hear me now?**"

around the world while also making us think of the importance of our civil liberties and being heard as we discuss our rights and freedoms. Soon after his verified account opened, Snowden had more than 70,000 followers. As of February 2013, his account, @Snowden, has almost three million followers. Snowden follows only one other account on Twitter—the NSA.

Although Snowden is still wanted by the United States government, he has done much in his years exiled in Russia to gain the approval of the public. His speaking engagements and work protecting the privacy of individuals and journalists continues.

CHAPTER NINE

Snowden in Popular Culture

The compelling story of Edward Snowden very quickly found its way into America's media and culture. In the few years that followed his NSA leaks, Edward Snowden appeared in news articles, books, news reports, television biopics, art, video games, Twitter tweets, viral memes, documentaries, and a feature film by director Oliver Stone. An Edward Snowden action figure is even available for purchase online. With Snowden's story still unfolding, there is sure to be more Snowden-related references in American popular culture and a continued recognition of the people who worked to bring Snowden's story to light—filmmaker Laura Poitras and journalist Glenn Greenwald.

Films by Laura Poitras

Long before anyone even knew who Edward Snowden was, people were already hard at work uncovering the truth about mass surveillance, whistleblowers, and civil liberties injustices.

The 2016 biopic film *Snowden* was directed by Oliver Stone and starred Joseph Gordon-Levitt. The film depicts Snowden throughout his career in the US intelligence community, culminating with his famed NSA leaks to reporters in Hong Kong.

87

While Snowden was still anonymous and working for the CIA and NSA, documentary filmmaker, journalist, and artist Laura Poitras had been busy crafting award-winning documentary films about the United States after the terrorist attacks on September 11, 2001. Before ever meeting Snowden, Poitras had already been placed on a secret US watchlist and subjected to US government detentions, surveillance, and scrutiny. She was detained at airports and had personal items taken from her because of her revealing documentary films. As a result, she had taken steps to protect herself and her work by adopting encryption methods.[1] She also spoke to Glenn Greenwald, who eventually reported in 2012 about the interrogation she was subjected to in the online magazine *Salon*.[2] Since early 2013, when Poitras first learned about Snowden's files, she kept the information confidential.

Poitras's first film about post-9/11 America, *My Country, My Country*, was released in 2006. According to Poitras's Praxis Films website, *My Country, My Country* "tells the story of Dr. Riyadh, an Iraqi doctor, father of six and Sunni political candidate. An outspoken critic of the US occupation, he is equally passionate about the need to establish democracy in Iraq, arguing that Sunni participation in the January 2005 elections is essential."[3] *My Country, My Country* was nominated for the Academy Award for best documentary film.

Poitras's second film about post-9/11 America, *The Oath*, was released in 2010. According to IMDB, *The Oath* "tells the story of two men whose fateful encounter in 1996 set them on a course of events that led them to Afghanistan, Osama bin Laden, 9/11, Guantanamo, and the US Supreme Court."[4] *The Oath* won many awards, including the Gotham Award for best documentary, the Sundance Film Festival award for best cinematography, and the Cinema Eye Honors Directing Award.

After first meeting Edward Snowden in the hotel room in Hong Kong, Poitras filmed their entire interview and eventually used the footage in a film called *Citizenfour*, which was released in 2014 and chronicles the interaction that she and Glenn Greenwald had with Snowden in Hong Kong in 2013 as he handed over the classified documents that proved the NSA's mass surveillance. *Citizenfour* is the third film in Poitras's 9/11

Astro Noise—Laura Poitras Art Installation

Astro Noise was an art exhibit at the Whitney Museum of American Art by artist, filmmaker, and journalist Laura Poitras. The installation exhibit featured new work about many of the modern concerns of American society, including the war on terror, mass surveillance, the Guantánamo Bay prison, torture, and the US drone program. According to the Whitney website, "The title, Astro Noise, refers to the faint background disturbance of thermal radiation left over from the Big Bang and is the name Edward Snowden gave to an encrypted file containing evidence of mass surveillance by the National Security Agency that he shared with Poitras in 2013."[5] The exhibit was Poitras's first solo museum exhibition, and it ran from February 5 to May 1, 2016.

trilogy. *Citizenfour* won many awards, including the Academy Award for Best Documentary, Emmy Award for Exceptional Merit in Documentary Filmmaking, and the British Academy Film and Television Award (BAFTA) for best documentary.

Oliver Stone

In 2016, the award-winning and controversial filmmaker Oliver Stone released a biopic film on Edward Snowden, simply titled *Snowden*. The film takes a subjective and dramatized view at Snowden's life before, during, and immediately after he disclosed top-secret files on NSA mass surveillance. The film starred Joseph Gordon-Levitt as Edward Snowden, Shailene Woodley as Lindsay Mills, Zachary Quinto as Glenn Greenwald, and Melissa Leo as Laura Poitras.

During the production of the film, Stone met with Snowden in Moscow, as well as journalist Greenwald and filmmaker Poitras. Stone also talked about the film before its release at the 2016 San Diego Comic Con. According to the *New York Times*, "Mr. Stone told attendees that his film was "a larger-than-life story of what is happening right now under our noses, and it affects the majority of you, this audience."[6] *Snowden* premiered at the Toronto International Film Festival on September 9, 2016, and was released in theaters on September 16, 2016.

Oliver Stone has been no stranger to tackling controversial film subjects, especially ones related to injustices by the United States government and conspiracies. Stone's 1986 Vietnam War film, *Platoon*, won the Academy Award for best picture, best director, best sound, and best film editing. Another controversial film by Stone was his 1991 film, *JFK*, which explored a possible conspiracy and mystery surrounding the November 22, 1963, assassination of President John F. Kennedy. *JFK* was nominated for numerous Academy

Conspiracy Theories

A conspiracy theory is an idea that an event or occurrence was the intentional result of planning by a group with harmful intentions. Some popular conspiracy theories include the idea that the murder of President John F. Kennedy was planned by the government and that the Americans landing on the moon never really happened. Most conspiracy theories are dismissed as false and ridiculous claims.

The television series *The X-Files* deals with one of the wildest conspiracy theories of all—that the government is keeping alien and UFO encounters secret from its citizens. In one episode, there is even a mention of Edward Snowden. In an episode titled "Founder's Mutation," the main character, Fox Mulder, is threatened not to disclose government secrets. He responded, "I'm familiar with Edward Snowden."[7]

Several conspiracy theories surround Edward Snowden. One is that Snowden is a Russian double agent. Another is that Snowden is a deep undercover agent for the NSA, purposely giving out false information so Americans will never know the truth. Like all conspiracy theories, there is no proof of any of the theories surrounding Edward Snowden.

Awards and won in the categories of best cinematography and best film editing.

Other Media

The video game industry is extremely popular and also quick to embrace fresh and dynamic news stories. The theme of Edward Snowden quickly found its way into the video game market. Now you can play as Edward Snowden and collect data, steal files, and evade capture or detection by the NSA. The games *Data Dealer* and *Snowden's Leak: The Game* are both small, independent games that are played on internet browsers. Two other video games, *Snowden Run 3D* and *Snowden Saga— Escape from Den of Iniquity*, are both available for mobile phones.

Edward Snowden has even become the subject of a comic book. *Beyond: Edward Snowden* was released on May 21, 2014, in print and digital editions. The comic, which focuses on Snowden's motivations for leaking NSA secrets, was published by Bluewater Productions. The comic was written by Valerie D'Orazio and illustrated by Dan Lauer. In an interview with *Business Insider*, D'Orazio said, "I've always had an interest in current events and media, and I've always wanted to write a comic book that acted as a bridge between geek culture and the mainstream . . . Snowden was perfect for this since he came from geek culture himself."[8]

> "I'm familiar with Edward Snowden."

Other artistic creations were also inspired or related to Edward Snowden. *Killswitch* is a 2014 documentary film about the internet. Edward Snowden is featured in part of the film. *Terminal F/Chasing Edward Snowden* is a 2014 documentary film about Edward Snowden and the journalists who helped uncover his story.

"Snowed In" is a song from musician Big Data on his 2015 debut album, *2.0.* Edward Snowden and the NSA inspired the song's lyrics. The song features Rivers Cuomo from the music group Weezer.

"Prison Ship Martyrs' Monument 2.0" is a 100-pound (45 kilograms), 4-foot (1.2 meters) tall bust sculpture of Edward Snowden that was illegally placed in Fort Greene Park in Brooklyn on April 6, 2015. Artists Jeff Greenspan and Andrew Tider created the sculpture. It was quickly removed and seized by New York City park officials. The following morning, a group of artists projected a hologram of Snowden at the same location for about twenty minutes.[9] The confiscated sculpture was eventually returned to the artists on May 6, 2015.[10] On February 17, 2016, the sculpture was displayed at the Brooklyn Museum in the Sackler Center for Feminist Art for the Agitprop! exhibition.

"Exit" is a song by musician Jean-Michel Jarre from his 2016 album, *Electronica Volume II: The Heart of Noise.* The six-minute song features Edward Snowden speaking and giving his opinions about mass surveillance. According to an interview with *Rolling Stone* magazine, Snowden said, "I've always appreciated electronic music. The melodies that I remember with most fondness are actually from video games where they generate 8-bit

Artists placed a sculpture of Edward Snowden in Brooklyn's Fort Greene Park on part of the Prison Ship Martyrs Monument in 2015. The New York City Parks Department covered the sculpture with a blue tarp before removing it.

music, and those kinds of chiptunes have really made a resurgence in modern musical culture today . . . And I think people like Jean Michel are the ones who really popularized that and made that possible for us to appreciate it as more than just sounds, as more than just background, but as actual culture."[11] Jarre traveled to Russia to meet Snowden and record his vocals for the song.

Edward Snowden and his leaked NSA files on mass surveillance continue to inspire artists, writers, musicians, journalists, filmmakers, and ordinary citizens from around the globe. Street art, fliers, and internet memes continue to emerge in popular culture, all inspired by Edward Snowden. The real-life Edward Snowden story is far from over, and his impact on popular culture will likely continue for a very long time.

CHAPTER TEN

The Future

· · · · · · · · · · · · ·

On January 20, 2017, Donald Trump was sworn in as the forty-fifth president of the United States of America. In the weeks that followed, there was much new news and speculation regarding Edward Snowden. Will he stay in Russia forever? Will he return to the United States? Will President Vladimir Putin hand him over to the United States as part of a deal? Many questions remain, and with Snowden continuing to speak out via video and tweets, the story is far from being over.

Presidential Reactions

On November 18, 2016, President Obama commented that he was not going to pardon Edward Snowden. Obama spoke at length with the German newspaper *Der Spiegel* as well as the German broadcaster ARD. Klaus Brinkbäumer and Sonia Seymour Mikich conducted the interview with President Obama. The interview covered a lot, but just before the interview was over, Obama was asked about Edward Snowden and if he intended to pardon him before his presidency was up.

Obama replied, "I can't pardon somebody who hasn't gone before a court and presented themselves, so that's not something that I would comment on at this point. I think that Mr. Snowden raised some legitimate concerns. How he did it was something that did not follow the procedures and practices of our intelligence community. If everybody took the approach that I make my own decisions about these issues, then it would

Death of Snowden?

Rumors that Edward Snowden was dead or had been killed began to circulate in the summer of 2016. On August 3, 2016, Snowden's Twitter account, @Snowden, had a mysterious tweet saying, "It's time." This cryptic tweet led some to speculate that Snowden was perhaps dead or had been kidnapped. Then on August 5, 2016, a mysterious sixty-four-character hex-code appeared on Snowden's Twitter account, "ffdae96f8dd292374a966ec8b57d9cc680ce1d2 3cb7072c522efe32a1a7e34b0." Some speculated that the code was perhaps a "dead man's switch" to release more files in the event of Snowden's death or kidnapping.[1] By August 9, 2016, Snowden's lawyer, Anatoly Kucherena, reported to the Russian state news agency RIA Novosti, "I can authoritatively say that he [Snowden] is alive and well, he is living in Russia and is busy with his favourite work."[2] Journalist Glenn Greenwald also posted to Twitter and announced that Snowden was fine.[3]

be very hard to have an organized government or any kind of national security system. At the point at which Mr. Snowden wants to present himself before the legal authorities and make his arguments or have his lawyers make his arguments, then I think those issues come into play."[4]

Obama ended the interview by expressing his confidence in the intelligence community and added that if our privacy was guaranteed and protected 100 percent, then our security would be compromised. Obama left office pardoning many people, but not Edward Snowden.[5]

President Donald Trump has been even less sympathetic toward Edward Snowden than President Obama. After news of Edward Snowden's NSA leaks first became news, then presidential candidate Donald Trump talked to Fox News. When asked about Snowden, he replied, "I think Snowden is a terrible threat. I think he's a terrible traitor and you know what we used to do in the good old days when we were a strong country? You know what we used to do to traitors, right?"

Eric Bolling of Fox News replied, "Well, you killed them, Donald."

Donald Trump continued, "This guy is really doing damage to this country, and he's also making us looks like dopes," Trump said. "We can't allow this guy to go out there and give out all our secrets and also embarrass us at every level. We should get him back and get him back now."[6]

Before becoming president, Trump also posted about Snowden on Twitter. On October 30, 2013, Trump

On January 20, 2017, Donald J. Trump was sworn in as the forty-fifth president of the United States. While he was campaigning for office, Trump had spoken out against Edward Snowden and condemned his actions.

• • • • • • • • • • • • • • • • • • • •

tweeted, "Snowden is a spy who should be executed—but if . . . he could reveal Obama's records, I might become a major fan."[7] Trump was referring to the controversy over the then president's birth certificate, which was questioned by some people who incorrectly believed that Obama was not born in the United States.

Donald Trump went on to become the forty-fifth president and still continues to post on Twitter regularly. Edward Snowden eventually commented on President Trump's presidency from a private search engine in Russia, StartPage. "We should not fear a Donald Trump, rather we should build it ourselves,"[8] Snowden said, referring to citizens' need to push for the desired changes in policy, mass surveillance, and civil liberties.

> "I don't know if the rumors are true. But I can tell you this: I am not afraid."

The next news to surface about Edward Snowden came about one month after Donald Trump became president of the United Sates. On February 10, 2017, NBC News reported, "US intelligence has collected information that Russia is considering turning over Edward Snowden as a 'gift' to President Donald Trump." A senior US official reported the information to NBC News and claimed to have "analyzed a series of highly sensitive intelligence reports detailing Russian deliberations and who says a Snowden handover is one of various ploys to 'curry favor' with Trump."[9]

The same day Snowden reacted to the news on his Twitter account, @Snowden, pointing to the news as proof that he was not a spy for Russian or another government. Snowden tweeted, "Finally: irrefutable evidence that I never cooperated with Russian intel. No country trades away spies, as the rest would fear they're next."[10]

Snowden continued to post on Twitter regarding the rumor. "I don't know if the rumors are true. But I can tell you this: I am not afraid. There are things that must be said no matter the consequence. Don't be afraid. Be ready. There are more of us than them."[11] The news was quickly dismissed by many news organizations as just speculation, with no real proof.

The Next Edward Snowden. . .

Who will be the next Edward Snowden and blow the whistle on some form of wrongdoing, illegal activity, or injustice around the world? The unknown person could come from any part of the United Sates or any country from around the world.

National counterintelligence executive William Evanina spoke to the *Guardian* in 2016 regarding the intelligence community policing itself to prevent another Snowden-like leak from happening in the future. While confident that security has been tightened to prevent another large leak from happening, Evanina said, "To no extent are we capable of stopping someone from doing damage who wants to. It's not possible. . .The same way you can't stop someone from starting a fire who wants to be an arsonist."[12]

Another whistleblower will surely emerge at some point. Will he or she help society or damage our security? Only time will tell.

The Future for Snowden

Edward Snowden's story is not over. News continues to surface. Under President Donald Trump, US foreign policy continues to change and evolve rapidly, especially with Russia, where Snowden is currently living.

Snowden continues to post on Twitter. His @Snowden Twitter bio states, "I used to work for the government. Now I work for the public. President at @FreedomofPress."

Edward Snowden continues to communicate via video feed at conferences and interviews around the world. At the 2017 CeBIT Technology Trade Fair in Hanover, Germany, Snowden denied having any connection to the Russian government.

Some of Snowden's tweets are meant to request help for people in need. For example, four families that helped him seek shelter as he was leaving Hong Kong in 2013 were in danger of being pursued by the Sri Lankan government for what they did. Snowden reached out to people on social media to raise money to help them find a new and safe place to live.[13]

Snowden also makes appearances via teleconference. CeBIT, which stands for, Computer Electronics Bureau

Information and Telecommunication, is an annual international five-day computer trade fair and expo. Snowden appeared at this conference in 2017 and answered questions posted for him ahead of time.[14]

While much of the public has embraced Edward Snowden as a courageous hero who stood up to the NSA and the United States government to expose the truth, there are many inside the US government who do not share this view. Many people feel Snowden will, eventually, return to the United States to face a trial. Many others believe in Snowden's actions, and feel they are justified and he should be pardoned or excused. Political cartoons, street art, T-shirts, posters, banners, and sculptures of Edward Snowden continue to appear around the world. Whether right or wrong, good or bad, Edward Snowden has become a symbol in our time—Snowden represents the lone individual against government mass surveillance.

Now that Edward Snowden has become so well known, no matter what happens to him in the future, the whole world will surely be watching.

Chronology

1952 President Harry Truman starts the NSA on November 4.

1975 The existence of the NSA first becomes known to the public.

1983 Edward Joseph Snowden is born on November 4 in Elizabeth City, North Carolina.

1997 Snowden graduates from junior high school and starts his freshman year at Arundel High School.

2001 Terrorist attack on the Pentagon, right outside the NSA, occurs on September 11. In December, Snowden starts chatting online and begins posting comments in a technology chat room called Ars Technica.

2004 Snowden joins the army reserves and begins basic training at Fort Benning, Georgia, on May 7. He is discharged on September 28.

2006 Snowden is hired by the Central Intelligence Agency and begins his career in intelligence.

2009 Snowden leaves the CIA in February.

2012 Snowden first contacts the *Guardian* freelance journalist Glenn Greenwald in December.

2013 Director of national intelligence James Clapper testifies before Congress in a public hearing in March. That same month, Snowden begins working for another NSA contractor at Booz Allen Hamilton. In April, Snowden and his girlfriend, Lindsay Mills, move into a new rented home in Hawaii. On May 20, Snowden leaves the United States and travels to Hong Kong to meet Glenn Greenwald and Laura Poitras. Snowden,

Greenwald, and Poitras meet for the first time on June 3. On June 6, Greenwald's first news article about Snowden's disclosures about the NSA is published by the *Guardian*. On June 7, journalist Barton Gellman and Laura Poitras publish an article in the *Washington Post* about a top-secret government program, code-named PRISM, based on information from Snowden. On June 11, Snowden is fired from his employer Booz Allen Hamilton. The United States government revokes Snowden's passport on June 23. Russian president Vladimir Putin holds a news conference on June 25, confirming that Snowden is in the "transit area" of the Sheremetyevo International Airport. Snowden applies for asylum in Russia at the consular office of Moscow's Sheremetyevo Airport on June 30. On November 1, Snowden writes a short article for the German periodical *Der Spiegel*.

2014 *Citizenfour*, the third film in Laura Poitras's 9/11 trilogy, is released. In February, Snowden joins the board of the nonprofit Freedom of the Press Foundation, located in San Francisco, California. On March 10, Snowden makes his first video appearance at the South by Southwest (SXSW) Conference and Festivals in Austin, Texas.

2015 Snowden opens a Twitter account in September. On June 2, 2015, President Barack Obama signs the Freedom Act into law.

2016 The Oliver Stone film *Snowden* is released in theaters on September 16.

2017 On February 10, NBC News reports that "US intelligence has collected information that Russia is considering turning over Edward Snowden as a 'gift' to President Donald Trump."

2020 Snowden's asylum in Russia is set to expire.

Chapter Notes

Introduction

1. Micah Lee, "Ed Snowden Taught Me to Smuggle Secrets Past Incredible Danger. Now I Teach You," The Intercept, October 28, 2014. https://theintercept.com/2014/10/28/smuggling-snowden-secrets.

2. Peter Finn and Sari Horwitz, "US Charges Snowden with Espionage," *Washington Post*, June 21, 2013. https://www.washingtonpost.com/world/national-security/us-charges-snowden-with-espionage/2013/06/21/507497d8-dab1-11e2-a016-92547bf094cc_story.html?utm_term=.4afd3c8e4df1.

3. Sarah Childress, "How the NSA Spying Programs Have Changed Since Snowden," PBS, February 9, 2015. http://www.pbs.org/wgbh/frontline/article/how-the-nsa-spying-programs-have-changed-since-snowden.

Chapter 1: Edward Who?

1. Bryan Burrough, Sarah Ellison, and Suzanna Andrews, "The Snowden Saga: A Shadowland of Secrets and Light," *Vanity Fair*, May 2014, http://www.vanityfair.com/news/politics/2014/05/edward-snowden-politics-interview.

2. Edward Jay Epstein, *How America Lost Its Secrets: Edward Snowden, the Man and the Theft* (New York, NY: Knopf, 2017), p. 15.

3. Ibid.

4. Burrough, Ellison, and Andrews.

5. "Edward Snowden's Father Full Interview w/ Eric Bolling on Fox - 6/17/13 - Lonnie Snowden," https://www.youtube.com/watch?v=A4c6WWvBraQ.

6. Burrough, Ellison, and Andrews.

7. Carol D. Leonnig, Jenna Johnson, and Marc Fisher, "Tracking Edward Snowden, from a Maryland Classroom to a Hong Kong Hotel," *Washington Post*, June 15, 2013, https://www.washingtonpost.com/world/national-security/tracking-edward-snowden-from-a-maryland-classroom-to-a-hong-kong-hotel/2013/06/15/420aedd8-d44d-11e2-b05f-3ea3f0e7bb5a_story.html?utm_term=.fd3e0b083746.

8. Ibid.

9. Ibid.

10. Lizzie Plaugic, "Edward Snowden Made a Song with Electronic Musician Jean-Michel Jarre," The Verge, April 15, 2016, http://www.theverge.com/2016/4/15/11437618/edward-snowden-jean-michel-jarre-song-exit.

11. "Edward Snowden," wired.com, August 2014, https://www.wired.com/2014/08/edward-snowden.

12. Leonnig, Johnson, and Fisher.

13. Luke Harding, "How Edward Snowden Went from a Loyal NSA Contractor to Whistleblower," *Guardian*, February 1, 2014, https://www.theguardian.com/world/2014/feb/01/edward-snowden-intelligence-leak-nsa-contractor-extract.

14. Garance Franke-Ruta, "Meet Edward Snowden, the NSA Whistleblower," *Atlantic*, June 2013, https://www.theatlantic.com/politics/archive/2013/06/meet-edward-snowden-the-nsa-whistleblower/276688.

15. Burrough, Ellison, and Andrews.

Chapter 2: Military and Intelligence

1. "Edward Snowden," wired.com, August 2014, https://www.wired.com/2014/08/edward-snowden.

2. "Rear Admiral Edward J. Barrett: Chief of Systems United States Coast Guard," US Coast Guard, http://www.uscg.mil/history/people/Flags/BarrettEBio.pdf.

3. Ashley Alman, "Edward Snowden Reflects on 9/11: I Take the Threat of Terrorism Seriously," *Huffington Post*, May 28, 2014, http://www.huffingtonpost.com/2014/05/28/edward-snowden-september-11_n_5407692.html.

4. "Edward Snowden," wired.com, August 2014, https://www.wired.com/2014/08/edward-snowden.

5. "Combat Special Forces Candidate," goarmy.com, http://www.goarmy.com/careers-and-jobs/browse-career-and-job-categories/combat/special-forces-candidate.html.

6. Edward Jay Epstein, *How America Lost Its Secrets: Edward Snowden, the Man and the Theft* (New York, NY: Knopf, 2017), p. 17.

7. Spencer Ackerman, "Edward Snowden Did Enlist for Special Forces, US Army Confirms," *Guardian*, June 10, 2013, https://www.theguardian.com/world/2013/jun/10/edward-snowden-army-special-forces.

8. "Edward Snowden," wired.com, August 2014, https://www.wired.com/2014/08/edward-snowden.

9. "Edward Snowden: Computer Programmer (1983-)," biography.com, http://www.biography.com/people/edward-snowden-21262897#early-years.

10. Epstein, p. 18.

11. "Edward Snowden," wired.com, August 2014, https://www.wired.com/2014/08/edward-snowden.

12. Luke Harding, *The Snowden Files: The Inside Story of the World's Most Wanted Man* (New York, NY: Vintage Books, 2014), p. 24.

13. Harding, pp. 33–35.

14. Eric Schmitt, "C.I.A. Warning on Snowden in '09 Said to Slip Through the Cracks," *The New York Times*, October 10, 2013, http://www.nytimes.com/2013/10/11/us/cia-

warning-on-snowden-in-09-said-to-slip-through-the-cracks.html.

15. "Edward Snowden," wired.com, August 2014, https://www.wired.com/2014/08/edward-snowden.

16. Harding, pp. 33–35.

Chapter 3: Hong Kong

1. Lee Ferran, "America's Top Spy James Clapper: 'I Made a Mistake but I Did Not Lie," ABC News, February 17, 2016, http://abcnews.go.com/US/americas-top-spy-james-clapper-made-mistake-lie/story?id=37003608.

2. Nick Gass, "White House: Snowden 'Is Not a Whistleblower,'" Politico, September 2016, http://www.politico.com/story/2016/09/edward-snowden-not-whistleblower-earnest-228163.

3. Ken Dilanian and Corky Siemaszko, "Director of National Intelligence James Clapper Resigns," NBC News, November 17, 2016, http://www.nbcnews.com/news/us-news/director-national-intelligence-james-clapper-resigns-n685301.

4. Luke Harding, *The Snowden Files: The Inside Story of the World's Most Wanted Man* (New York, NY: Vintage Books, 2014), p. 54.

5. Andrea Peterson, "The Five Things You Need to Know About Snowden's First US Television Interview," *Washington Post*, May 29, 2014, https://www.washingtonpost.com/news/the-switch/wp/2014/05/29/the-five-things-you-need-to-know-about-snowdens-first-u-s-television-interview/?utm_term=.592341fbd491.

6. Harding, pp. 57, 60.

7. Luke Harding, "How Edward Snowden Went from Loyal NSA Contractor to Whistleblower," *Guardian*, May 29, 2014, https://www.washingtonpost.com/news/the-switch/wp/2014/05/29/the-five-things-you-need-to-know-

about-snowdens-first-u-s-television-interview/?utm_
term=.592341fbd491.

8. Ibid.

9. Luke Harding, *The Snowden Files: The Inside Story of the World's Most Wanted Man* (New York, NY: Vintage Books, 2014).

10. Ibid.

11. "'Right Out of a Spy Movie': Glenn Greenwald on First Secret Meeting with NSA Leaker Edward Snowden," Democracy Now!, May 14, 2014, https://www.democracynow.org/2014/5/14/right_out_of_a_spy_movie.

12. Luke Harding, "How Edward Snowden Went from Loyal NSA Contractor to Whistleblower," *Guardian*, February 2014, https://www.theguardian.com/world/2014/feb/01/edward-snowden-intelligence-leak-nsa-contractor-extract.

13. "Edward Snowden Makes the Best Rebuttal to 'I Have Nothing to Hide'" Daily Kos, March 27, 2016, http://www.dailykos.com/story/2016/3/27/1506887/-Edward-Snowden-makes-the-best-rebuttal-to-I-have-nothing-to-hide.

14. Luke Harding, "How Edward Snowden Went from Loyal NSA Contractor to Whistleblower,".

15. *CitizenFour*, film by Laura Poitras.

16. Ewen MacAskill, Julian Borger, Nick Hopkins, Nick Davis, and James Ball, "GCHQ Taps Fibre-Optic Cables for Secret Access to Worlds' Communications," *Guardian*, June 21, 2013, https://www.theguardian.com/uk/2013/jun/21/gchq-cables-secret-world-communications-nsa.

17. Glenn Greenwald, "NSA Collecting Phone Records of Millions of Verizon Customers Daily," *Guardian*, June 6, 2013, https://www.theguardian.com/world/2013/jun/06/nsa-phone-records-verizon-court-order.

Chapter 4: The News Gets Reported

1. Barton Gellman, "US, British Intelligence Mining Data from Nine US Internet Companies in Broad Secret Program," *Washington Post*, June 7, 2013, https://www.washingtonpost.com/investigations/us-intelligence-mining-data-from-nine-us-internet-companies-in-broad-secret-program/2013/06/06/3a0c0da8-cebf-11e2-8845-d970ccb04497_story.html?utm_term=.bc088f8be7f2.

2. Ed O'Keefe, "Transcript: Dianne Feinstein, Saxby, Chambliss Explain, Defend NSA Phone Records Program," *Washington Post*, June 6, 2013, https://www.washingtonpost.com/news/post-politics/wp/2013/06/06/transcript-dianne-feinstein-saxby-chambliss-explain-defend-nsa-phone-records-program/?utm_term=.17c1e3856915.

3. Gregory Korte, "CIA, NSA Contractor Admits to Leaking Secret Programs," *USA Today*, June 9, 2013, http://www.usatoday.com/story/news/nation/2013/06/09/contractor-admits-to-leaking-to-guardian/2405723.

4. Ibid.

5. Dana Bash and Tom Cohen, "Officials Cite Thwarted Plots, Oversight in Defending Surveillance," CNN, June 19, 2013, http://www.cnn.com/2013/06/18/politics/nsa-leaks/index.html?on.cnn=1.

6. Kevin Liptak, "Obama Bristles at Suggestion He's Shifted on Snooping," CNN, June 18, 2013, http://www.cnn.com/2013/06/17/politics/obama-nsa-interview/index.html.

7. Glenn Greenwald, Ewen MacAskill, and Laura Poitras, "Edward Snowden: The Whistleblower Behind the NSA Surveillance Revelations," *Guardian*, June 11, 2013, https://www.theguardian.com/world/2013/jun/09/edward-snowden-nsa-whistleblower-surveillance.

8. Ibid.

9. Bash and Cohen.

10. Peter Finn and Sari Horwitz, "US Charges Snowden with Espionage," *Washington Post*, June 21, 2013, https://www.washingtonpost.com/world/national-security/us-charges-snowden-with-espionage/2013/06/21/507497d8-dab1-11e2-a016-92547bf094cc_story.html?utm_term=.52fc216195b5.

11. "Edward Snowden Leaves Hong Kong on Moscow Flight," BBC, June 23, 2013, http://www.bbc.com/news/world-asia-china-23019414.

12. "China's Xinhua news agency condemns US 'cyber-attacks,'" BBC, June 23, 2013. http://www.bbc.com/news/world-asia-23018938.

13. "Edward Snowden Leaves Hong Kong on Moscow Flight," BBC, June 23, 2013, http://www.bbc.com/news/world-asia-china-23019414.

14. Jethro Mullen and Michael Pearson, "Snowden a 'Free Man' in Moscow Airport, Russian President Says," CNN, June 25, 2013, http://www.cnn.com/2013/06/25/politics/nsa-leak.

15. Ellen Barry, Michael D. Shear, and William Neuman, "Obama Seeks to Play Down Snowden's Import," *New York Times*, June 27, 2013, http://www.nytimes.com/2013/06/28/world/snowden.html.

16. "White House Urges Moscow to Expel Snowden to US," *South China Morning Post*, http://www.scmp.com/news/hong-kong/article/1268378/white-house-urges-moscow-expel-snowden-us.

17. "Ecuador's Correa Says Biden Asked Him to Deny Edward Snowden Asylum," *Guardian*, https://www.theguardian.com/world/2013/jun/29/edward-snowden-biden-correa-talks.

18. Miriam Elder, "Snowden Applies for Political Asylum in Russia—and 20 Other Countries," *Guardian*, https://

www.theguardian.com/world/2013/jul/01/putin-snowden-remain-russia-offer.

Chapter 5: Many Questions, Many Reactions

1. James Glanz and Andrew W. Lehren, "N.S.A. Spied on Allies, Aid Groups and Businesses," *New York Times*, December 20, 2013, http://www.nytimes.com/2013/12/21/world/nsa-dragnet-included-allies-aid-groups-and-business-elite.html.

2. "'Explosive' NSA Spying Reports Are Imminent," Spiegel Online, July 19, 2013, http://www.spiegel.de/international/world/journalist-says-explosive-reports-coming-from-snowden-data-a-912034.html.

3. Michael B. Kelley, "Snowden Took as Many as 200,000 NSA Documents, and That's Very Troubling," *Business Insider*, November 14, 2013, http://www.businessinsider.com/snowden-took-as-many-as-200000-nsa-documents-2013-11.

4. Eli Lake, "Greenwald: Snowden's Files Are Out There If 'Anything Happens' to Him," Daily Beast, June 25, 2013, http://www.thedailybeast.com/articles/2013/06/25/greenwald-snowden-s-files-are-out-there-if-anything-happens-to-him.html.

5. Michael B. Kelley, "NSA: Snowden Stole 1.7 Million Classified Documents and Still Has Access to Most of Them," *Business Insider*, December 13, 2013, http://www.businessinsider.com/how-many-docs-did-snowden-take-2013-12.

6. David Ignatius, "Edward Snowden Took Less Than Previously Thought Says James Clapper," *Washington Post*, June 5, 2014, https://www.washingtonpost.com/opinions/edward-snowden-took-less-than-previously-thought-says-james-clapper/2014/06/05/054cb9f2-ecee-11e3-93d2-edd4be1f5d9e_story.html?hpid=z1&utm_term=.f53868022c36.

7. "Frank Serpico Biography: Law Enforcement (1936–)," biography.com, http://www.biography.com/people/frank-serpico-9542108.

8. "Inside the Tobacco Deal: Jeffrey Wigand," PBS, http://www.pbs.org/wgbh/pages/frontline/shows/settlement/timelines/wigand.html.

9. Charlie Savage, "Chelsea Manning to Be Released Early as Obama Commutes Sentence," *New York Times*, January 17, 2017, https://www.nytimes.com/2017/01/17/us/politics/obama-commutes-bulk-of-chelsea-mannings-sentence.html.

10. Kelley, "NSA: Snowden Stole 1.7 Million Classified Documents and Still Has Access to Most of Them."

11. James Glanz and Andrew W. Lehren, "NSA Spied on Allies, Aid Groups and Businesses," *New York Times*, December 20, 2013, http://www.nytimes.com/2013/12/21/world/nsa-dragnet-included-allies-aid-groups-and-business-elite.html.

12. James Ball, "NSA Monitored Calls of 35 World Leaders After US Official Handed Over Contacts," *Guardian*, October 25, 2013, https://www.theguardian.com/world/2013/oct/24/nsa-surveillance-world-leaders-calls.

13. "Readout of the President's Call with President Hollande of France," The White House, Office of the Press Secretary, October 21, 2013, https://obamawhitehouse.archives.gov/the-press-office/2013/10/21/readout-president-s-call-president-hollande-france.

14. Ian Traynor, Philip Oltermann, and Paul Lewis, "Angela Merkel's Call to Obama: Are You Bugging My Mobile Phone?," *Guardian*, October 24, 2013, https://www.theguardian.com/world/2013/oct/23/us-monitored-angela-merkel-german.

15. "Watergate Scandal," History, http://www.history.com/topics/watergate.

16. Lana Lam, "Snowden Sought Booz Allen Job to Gather Evidence on NSA Surveillance," *South China Morning Post*, June 24, 2013, http://www.scmp.com/news/hong-kong/article/1268209/snowden-sought-booz-allen-job-gather-evidence-nsa-surveillance.

17. Richard Esposito and Matthew Cole, "How Snowden Did It," NBC News, August 26, 2013, http://www.scmp.com/news/hong-kong/article/1268209/snowden-sought-booz-allen-job-gather-evidence-nsa-surveillance.

18. Eric Schmitt, "CIA Warning on Snowden in '09 to Slip Through the Cracks," *New York Times*, October 10, 2013, http://www.nytimes.com/2013/10/11/us/cia-warning-on-snowden-in-09-said-to-slip-through-the-cracks.html?partner=rss&emc=rss&smid=tw-nytimes.

19. Mavanee Anderson, "Who Is Ed Snowden? Friend Shares Memories, Offers Support for NSA Leaker," *Times Free Press*, June 12, 2013, http://www.timesfreepress.com/news/opinion/freepress/story/2013/jun/12/who-is-ed-snowden/110584.

Chapter 6: Hero or Traitor?

1. Edward Snowden, "Snowden: A Manifesto for the Truth," Global Research, http://www.globalresearch.ca/a-manifesto-for-the-truth/5356919.

2. "Edward Snowden Is a Hero Not a Traitor," Amnesty International, https://www.amnesty.org/en/get-involved/take-action/Edward-Snowden-hero-not-traitor.

3. Philip Giraldi, "Edward Snowden Is No Traitor," *American Conservative*, July 16, 2013, http://www.theamericanconservative.com/articles/edward-snowden-is-no-traitor.

4. Amanda Sakuma, "Democrats Split on Whether to Champion or Condemn Snowden," MSNBC, October 14, 2015, http://www.msnbc.com/msnbc/democratic-divisions-over-what-make-edward-snowden.

5. Douglas Rushkoff, "Edward Snowden Is a Hero," CNN, June 10, 2013, http://www.cnn.com/2013/06/10/opinion/rushkoff-snowden-hero.

6. Jim Newell, "Thousands Gather in Washington for Anti-NSA 'Stop Watching Us' Rally," Guardian, October 26, 2013, https://www.theguardian.com/world/2013/oct/26/nsa-rally-stop-watching-washington-snowden.

7. "Edward Snowden, Whistle-Blower," *New York Times*, January 1, 2014, https://www.nytimes.com/2014/01/02/opinion/edward-snowden-whistle-blower.html?_r=0.

8. Zachary Keck, "Yes, Edward Snowden Is a Traitor," *Diplomat*, December 21, 2013, http://thediplomat.com/2013/12/yes-edward-snowden-is-a-traitor.

9. Charles Moore, "Edward Snowden Is a Traitor, Just as Sure as George Blake Was," *Diplomat*, July 5, 2013, http://www.telegraph.co.uk/technology/internet-security/10162351/Edward-Snowden-is-a-traitor-just-as-surely-as-George-Blake-was.html.

10. Alyssa Newcomb, "AdBlock's Ironic Approach to World Day Against Cyber Censorship," ABC News, March 11, 2016, http://abcnews.go.com/Technology/adblocks-ironic-approach-world-day-cyber-censorship/story?id=37581011.

11. Joanna Walters, "Edward Snowden, Pussy Riot, and Ai Weiwei Are Partnering AdBlock to Protest Censorship," ABC News, March 11, 2016, http://mobile.businessinsider.com/adblock-campaign-protests-censorship-2016-3.

12. "Opinion Journal: Edward Snowden, Traitor," *Wall Street Journal*, September 16, 2016, http://www.wsj.com/video/opinion-journal-edward-snowden-traitor/0067807E-75F7-4C6A-B85C-61B295241FE7.html.

13. "Executive Summary of Review of the Unauthorized Disclosures of Former National Security Agency Contractor Edward Snowden," US House of

Representatives, September 15, 2016, https://intelligence.
house.gov/uploadedfiles/hpsci_snowden_review_-_
unclass_summary_-_final.pdf.

Chapter 7: The Snowden Effect

1. David E. Sanger, "US and Germany Fail to Reach a Deal on Spying," *New York Times*, May 1, 2014, https://www.nytimes.com/2014/05/02/world/europe/us-and-germany-fail-to-reach-a-deal-on-spying.html.

2. Mark Scott, "Irked by N.S.A, Germany Cancels Deal with Verizon," *New York Times*, June 26, 2014, https://www.nytimes.com/2014/06/27/business/angered-by-nsa-activities-germany-cancels-verizon-contract.html.

3. Associated Press, "Germany Signs No-Spy Deal with Blackberry After NSA Phone Tapping," *New York Daily News*, November 28, 2014, http://www.nydailynews.com/news/politics/germany-signs-no-spy-deal-blackberry-nsa-debacle-article-1.2026683.

4. Geir Moulson, "Angela Merkel, German Chancellor, Testifies on Alleged US Eavesdropping," *Washington Times*, February 16, 2017, http://www.washingtontimes.com/news/2017/feb/16/germanys-merkel-to-testify-before-parliament-nsa-p.

5. "'Spying Among Friends Unacceptable': Merkel Testifies on Alleged US Eavesdropping," *South China Morning Post*, February 16, 2017, http://www.scmp.com/news/world/europe/article/2071538/spying-among-friends-unacceptable-merkel-testifies-alleged-us.

6. Mary Beth Quirk, "Apple: We Won't Unlock Devices When the Police Ask, Because iOS8 Doesn't Let Us," Consumerist, September 18, 2014, https://consumerist.com/2014/09/18/apple-we-wont-unlock-devices-when-the-police-ask-because-ios-8-doesnt-let-us.

7. Allen McDuffee, "iPhone 6 Could Lock Out NSA, Law Enforcement," *Atlantic*, September 27, 2014, https://www.

theatlantic.com/technology/archive/2014/09/iphone-6-may-lock-out-nsa-law-enforcement/380865/.

8. Craig Timberg, "Newest Androids Will Join iPhones in Offering Default Encryption Blocking Police," *Atlantic*, September 18, 2014, https://www.washingtonpost.com/news/the-switch/wp/2014/09/18/newest-androids-will-join-iphones-in-offering-default-encryption-blocking-police/?utm_term=.99325ed3a495.

9. David E. Sanger and Brian X. Chen, "Signaling Post-Snowden Era, New iPhone Locks Out N.S.A," *New York Times*, September 26, 2014, https://www.nytimes.com/2014/09/27/technology/iphone-locks-out-the-nsa-signaling-a-post-snowden-era-.html.

10. "A Message to Our Customers," Apple, February 16, 2014, http://www.apple.com/customer-letter.

11. Mark Zuckerberg, "Facebook Post by Mark Zuckerberg," Facebook, https://www.facebook.com/zuck/posts/10100828955847631.

Chapter 8: Exile in Russia

1. "Edward Snowden: A Timeline," NBC News, http://www.nbcnews.com/feature/edward-snowden-interview/edward-snowden-timeline-n114871.

2. "Ex-NSA Contractor Snowden Finds Computer Job in Russia," Sputnik News, October 31, 2013, https://sputniknews.com/russia/20131031184453637-Fugitive-Ex-Contractor-Snowden-Finds-Computer-Job-in-Russia.

3. Barton Gellman, "Edward Snowden After Months of NSA Revelations Says His Mission's Accomplished," Washington Post, December 23, 2013, https://www.washingtonpost.com/world/national-security/edward-snowden-after-months-of-nsa-revelations-says-his-missions-accomplished/2013/12/23/49fc36de-6c1c-11e3-a523-fe73f0ff6b8d_story.html?Post%20

generic=%3Ftid%3Dsm_twitter_washingtonpost&utm_term=.88fb98878f36.

4. "Edward Snowden Speaks at SXSW Conference," Star Advertiser, March 10, 2014, http://www.staradvertiser.com/2014/03/10/breaking-news/edward-snowden-speaks-at-sxsw-conference.

5. Scott Shane, "Snowden Sees Some Victories, From a Distance," New York Times, May 19, 2015, https://www.nytimes.com/2015/05/20/world/europe/snowden-sees-some-victories-from-a-distance.html.

6. Ibid.

7. Michael Isikoff and Michael B. Kelley, "In Exile, Edward Snowden Rakes in Speaking Fees While Hoping for a Pardon," Yahoo News, August 11, 2016, https://www.yahoo.com/news/edward-snowden-making-most-digital-000000490.html?nhp=1.

8. Ibid.

9. Bill Schackner, "Snowden to Address Pitt Students via Video Stream from Russia," Pittsburgh Post-Gazette, January 11, 2017, http://www.post-gazette.com/news/education/2017/01/11/Snowden-to-address-Pitt-students-via-video-stream-from-Russia/stories/201701100176.

10. Stephanie Strasburg, "Edward Snowden Talks in Real Time with Pitt Students," Pittsburgh Post-Gazette, February 2, 2017, http://www.post-gazette.com/news/education/2017/02/02/Edward-Snowden-talks-in-real-time-with-Pitt-students/stories/201702020156.

11. Ashwini Sivaganesh and Amanda Reed, "Edward Snowden to Broadcast Live on Campus," Pitt News, January 9, 2017, http://pittnews.com/article/115254/news/ppc-hosts-edward-snowden-live-video-chat.

12. "About: Freedom of the Press Foundation's Missions, Values, and People," Freedom of the Press Foundation, https://freedom.press/about.

13. "Security Tools," Freedom of the Press Foundation, https://freedom.press/tools.

14. "US House of Representatives Permanent Select Committee on Intelligence," September 15, 2016, http://intelligence.house.gov/uploadedfiles/hpsci_members_letter_to_potus_re_snowden-15_sep_16.pdf.

15. John Gramlich and Kristen Bialik, "Obama Used Clemency Power More Often Than Any President Since Truman," Pew Research, January 20, 2017, http://www.pewresearch.org/fact-tank/2017/01/20/obama-used-more-clemency-power.

Chapter 9: Snowden in Popular Culture

1. Glenn Greenwald, *No Place to Hide* (London, UK: Picador, 2015), p. 5.

2. Glenn Greenwald, "US Filmmaker Repeatedly Detained at Border," Salon, April 8, 2012, http://www.salon.com/2012/04/08/u_s_filmmaker_repeatedly_detained_at_border.

3. *My Country, My Country*, Praxis Films, http://www.praxisfilms.org/films/my-country-my-country.

4. "The Oath (2010)," imdb.com, http://www.imdb.com/title/tt1522857/?ref_=nm_ov_bio_lk2.

5. "Laura Poitras: Astro Noise (Feb 5–May1, 2016)," Whitney, http://whitney.org/Exhibitions/LauraPoitras.

6. Brooks Barnes, "Oliver Stone's *Snowden* Gives Comic Con Its Moment of Gravity," *New York Times*, July 22, 2016, https://www.nytimes.com/2016/07/23/movies/oliver-stones-snowden-gives-comic-con-its-moment-of-gravity.html?mtrref=undefined&gwh=BE14BA51013BFA447EB1BF975C9BED64&gwt=pay.

7. Tim Martin, "The X Files, Episode 2: It's Getting Gruesome, Plus 4 Other Things We Learned," *Telegraph*, February 15, 2016, http://www.telegraph.co.uk/tv/2016/02/15/the-x-files-episode-2-its-getting-gruesome-plus-4-other-things-w.

8. Jeremy Bender, "Edward Snowden Will Soon Be a Comic Book Star," *Business Insider*, May 20, 2014, http://www.businessinsider.com/beyond-edward-snowden-marvel-comic-2014-5.

9. Jim Dwyer, "A Removed Snowden Sculpture Inspires a Hologram in Its Place," *New York Times*, April 7, 2015, https://www.nytimes.com/2015/04/08/nyregion/a-removed-snowden-sculpture-inspires-a-hologram-in-its-place.html?mtrref=undefined&gwh=461E3F5B01FA9CE53F26E58330961857&gwt=pay.

10. Dareh Gregorian, "Edward Snowden Bust Artists Recover Sculpture from the City," *New York Daily News*, May 6, 2015, http://www.nydailynews.com/new-york/brooklyn/edward-snowden-bust-artists-recover-sculpture-city-article-1.2212650.

11. Daniel Kreps, "Edward Snowden's New Job: Electronic Music Vocalist," *Rolling Stone*, April 15, 2016, http://www.rollingstone.com/music/news/edward-snowdens-new-job-electronic-music-vocalist-20160415.

Chapter 10: The Future

1. "Edward Snowden Tweets Cryptic Code: Was It a Dead Man's Switch?," Sputnik News, June 8, 2016, https://sputniknews.com/news/201608061044011551-snowden-twitter-leaks-dead-kidnapped.

2. "Snowden 'Not Dead' Says Lawyer," news.com.au, August 9, 2016, http://www.news.com.au/world/breaking-news/snowden-not-dead-says-lawyer/news-story/379942bc07b368b0fe8d280f8352cd32.

3. "Edward Snowden Not Dead: 'He's Fine' Says Glenn Greenwald After Mysterious Tweet," Sputnik News, July 8, 2016, https://sputniknews.com/military/201608071044016775-snowden-dead-man-switch-greenwald.

4. Klaus Brinkbaumer and Sonia Seymour Mikich, "We Could See More and More Divisions," Spiegel Online, November 18, 2016, http://www.spiegel.de/international/world/spiegel-interview-with-us-president-barack-obama-a-1122008.html.

5. Ibid.

6. Hadas Gold, "Trump Raises Death Penalty," Politico, http://www.politico.com/story/2013/07/donald-trump-edward-snowden-nsa-leak-093606.

7. Kyle Cheney, "Trump in 2013: He'd Be 'Major Fan' of Snowden If He Revealed Obama Records," Politico, July 27, 2016, http://www.politico.com/story/2016/07/donald-trump-hacking-edward-snowden-russia-226320.

8. Thomas Fox-Brewster, "Edward Snowden Says Don't Fear Donald Trump—Save Yourselves from Surveillance," Forbes, November 10, 2016, https://www.forbes.com/sites/thomasbrewster/2016/11/10/edward-snowden-pardon-president-donald-trump-pardon/#2492e2f61357.

9. Cynthia McFadden and William Arkin, "Russia Considers Returning Snowden to US to 'Curry Favor' with Trump: Official," CNBC, February 10, 2017, http://www.cnbc.com/2017/02/10/russia-eyes-sending-snowden-to-us-as-gift-to-trump-official-tells-nbc-news.html.

10. Olivia Solon, "Snowden Claims Report Russia May 'Gift' Him to Trump Proves He Is Not a Spy," Guardian, February 10, 2017, https://www.theguardian.com/us-news/2017/feb/10/edward-snowden-russia-trump-report.

11. Vickie Oliphant, "'I Am Not Afraid' Snowden Remains Defiant After Claims Putin Will Hand Him Over to Trump," Express, February 12, 2017, http://www.express.

co.uk/news/world/766295/Edward-Snowden-twitter-not-afraid-Vladimir-Putin-Russia-gift-Donald-Trump.

12. Patrick Tucker, "Can the NSA Stop the Next Snowden?" *Atlantic*, September 18, 2016, https://www.theatlantic.com/international/archive/2016/09/nsa-snowden/500345.

13. Rebecca Wright, "Refugees Who Sheltered Snowden Now Live in Fear in Hong Kong," CNN, February 26, 2017, http://www.cnn.com/2017/02/24/asia/hong-kong-snowden-refugees.

14. "America First? Edward Snowden at CeBIT 2017," CeBIT, February 2, 2017, http://www.cebit.de/en/register-plan/for-journalists/press-releases/pressreleases-deutsche-messe/america-first-edward-snowden-at-cebit-2017.xhtml.

Glossary

adversary Opponent.

arrest warrant Official document allowing for the arrest of an individual.

asylum The protection of a group or individual from danger.

clandestine Done in secret.

code Programming instructions for a computer system.

conspiracy theory A belief that events or circumstances are planned by a group with negative intentions.

dystopian Relating to an unpleasant or bad existence, usually in terms of government control.

encrypt To hide or conceal.

encryption software A type of computer software that makes data unreadable without being translated or decoded with a password.

espionage The practice of spying, typically by the government or military.

extradite To hand over a person accused of a crime.

hacking Gaining access to a computer system without permission.

latitude Freedom of thought.

metadata A set of computer data that gives information about other data.

pardon The act of forgiving or excusing someone for an offense.

whistleblower A person who informs authorities of an organization's wrongdoings.

wittingly Done with full awareness.

Further Reading

Books

Greenwald, Glenn. *No Place to Hide: Edward Snowden, the NSA, and the US Surveillance State.* New York, NY: Picador, 2015.

Harding, Luke. *The Snowden Files: The Inside Story of the World's Most Wanted Man.* New York, NY: Vintage, 2014.

Higgins, Melissa. *Edward Snowden: NSA Whistle-Blower.* North Mankato, MN: ABDO, 2016.

Snowden, Edward James. *Everything You Know About the Constitution Is Wrong.* Seattle, WA: CreateSpace Independent Publishing Platform, 2013.

Websites

National Security Agency
https://www.nsa.gov
Website of the NSA, the government agency that Edward Snowden revealed as performing illegal surveillance on the public.

National Whistleblower Center (NWC)
http://www.whistleblowers.org
Organization for the advocacy of whistleblowers.

Films

Citizenfour, by Laura Poitras (documentary)

Snowden, directed by Oliver Stone (drama)

Index